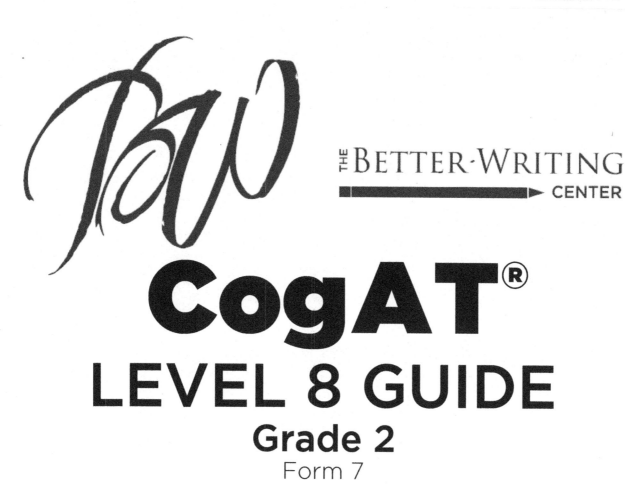

THE BETTER·WRITING CENTER

CogAT®
LEVEL 8 GUIDE
Grade 2
Form 7

By
Won Suh, J.D.
John S. Kim

Acknowledgement

I thank my coauthor John Kim for his hard work and near flawless execution of this book. At the time of this book's initial printing, John is a sophomore at the Thomas Jefferson High School for Science and Technology (my alma mater) and a long time student of mine—I've known him for so long, I sometimes forget that he's not a younger cousin or a nephew.

In my years of teaching, I have yet to find another student who has the same combination of integrity, intelligence, and magnanimity. As such, when I began to plan this CogAT® book, I had one of the most radical ideas I've had as an author and publisher: to give John an opportunity of a lifetime. (For whom this publication is more of an opportunity is debatable.)

This is saying a lot, as I have a business to run: it is imperative that every book published by The Better Writing Center is of the highest quality. I would have to be crazy to entrust the authorship of one of my books to anyone else, let alone a high school student, if I wasn't absolutely sure of his or her abilities. I was confident John could pull this off, and with this publication, I am now absolutely sure I made the right decision. With any luck (on my part), John will stick around to see his name adorn the covers of more of my books.

To say that John is my coauthor is to wholly give myself too much credit. John is the author. I tagged along for the ride and made final adjustments—very small adjustments—as needed to ensure the same high level of quality that parents have come to appreciate from my first two CogAT® books.

How to Use This Book

This book contains 3 primary components: a study guide with examples to help you help your child understand how to approach CogAT® questions, a full-length practice test, and answers and explanations.

If this is your child's first time preparing for the CogAT®, you may want to start with the study guide and then proceed to the practice test. But if your child is familiar with the CogAT®, then you may want to consider trying the practice test first and then going over the answers and explanations; the study guide may be wholly unnecessary. I included it for the benefit of you and your child, just in case.

Study Guide's Structure

The study guide is written for you, the parent, to help your child understand the approach he or she needs to take to solve CogAT®-style questions accurately and efficiently.

The study guide is comprised of 9 sections, one for each question type. Each of the 9 sections of the study guide is comprised of 3 main parts: Structure of the Problem, Tackling the Problem, and Drills. Read these carefully and work through the drills and example problems. The answer explanations for each drill will be provided after the drill.

Practice Test's Structure

The CogAT® is comprised of 3 subtests: Verbal Battery, Quantitative Battery, and Nonverbal Battery. Each subtest is further broken down into 3 sections, for a total of 9 sections. In this book, each page of each of these 9 sections contains 2 questions. This was a deliberate design decision to better maximize the amount of visual space per problem and thereby minimize any potential confusion and room for error.

Answer Key and Explanation's Structure

The answer key and explanations are located at the back of the book. Be sure to go over the explanations to get a full understanding of how to solve the questions with your child.

Thank you and good luck!

Won Suh
Author

Contents

FREE CONSULTATION

Thank you for your purchase. Your purchase entitles you to a complimentary hour of in-person private tutoring or academic consultation.* Just bring this book!

SCHEDULE YOUR CONSULTATION TODAY
won.suh@betterwritingcenter.com

*This offer is subject to scheduling and availability limitations and will be honored on a first come, first serve basis.

TUTORING OFFERED

LEARN FROM THE BEST. LEARN FROM THE AUTHOR.

TESTING	MATHEMATICS	SCIENCE	WRITING
CogAT	Algebra 1 & 2	Biology	School Assignments
SSAT	Geometry	Chemistry	AP History DBQs
SHSAT	Trigonometry	Physics	Personal Statements
ACT	Pre-calculus	Computer Science	Application Essays
SAT	AP Calculus AB & BC		

FIND THE BETTER WRITING CENTER

THE BETTER WRITING CENTER
7369 McWhorter Place
Suite 402
Annandale, Virginia 22003

STUDY Guide

Verbal Analogies Guide

Overview

There are 18 verbal analogies questions in the form 7, level 8 administration of the CogAT®. The student must completely fill in the bubble below the image he or she believes to be the correct answer.

Structure of the Verbal Analogies Questions

In verbal analogies questions, there are 4 squares, arranged in a 2-by-2 grid formation—that is, two squares on top and two squares on bottom. The answer choices will either be to the right or bottom of this 2-by-2 grid. The outline of a question is shown in the figure below.

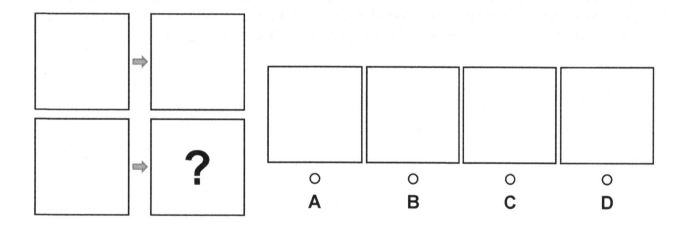

The images in the top two squares are somehow related or correlated to each other, so the images in the bottom two squares are also related to each other in a similar way.

The image in the bottom right square is not supplied and is instead replaced by a question mark. The goal of the question is to figure out which image from the answer choices replaces the question mark.

Tackling the Verbal Analogies Questions

To figure out which answer choice's image should replace the question mark, it is important to understand the relationship between the images in the top two squares of each problem. Study the top two squares in the grid.

Some common relationships are:

1. Synonyms and Antonyms
2. Use or Purpose
3. Cause and Effect
4. Characteristics and Traits in Common

What if the Answer is Not Obvious?

If there doesn't seem to be a relationship or correlation between the top two images, look instead for similarities between the images in the left squares. Then look for similarities in the image in the top right square and the images in the answer choices.

Verbal Analogies Drills

Thought Exercises

Directions: Imagine that the top left square is the first square (1), the top right square is the second (2), the bottom left square is the third (3), and the bottom right square is the fourth (4). Keeping this in mind, fill in the blanks with your own words to complete the analogy.

1. Hair (1) is to fur (2) as hand (3) is to _____ (4).

2. Car (1) is to road (2) as boat (3) is to _____ (4).

3. Pepsi (1) is to soda (2) as Barbie (3) is to _____ (4).

4. Quarter (1) is to dollar (2) as quart (3) is to _____ (4).

5. Eat (1) is to taste (2) as touch (3) is to _____ (4).

6. Remember (1) is to forget (2) as build (3) is to _____ (4).

7. Clear (1) is to clean (2) as murky (3) is to _____ (4).

8. Banana (1) is to long (2) as orange (3) is to _____ (4).

9. Cake (1) is to pie (2) as tea (3) is to _____ (4).

10. Thanksgiving (1) is to turkey (2) as Easter (3) is to _____ (4).

11. Pen (1) is to marker (2) as paper clip (3) is to _____ (4).

12. Red (1) is to stop (2) as green (3) is to _____ (4).

Example CogAT® Question

Directions: Fill in the circle belonging to the image that best completes the analogy.

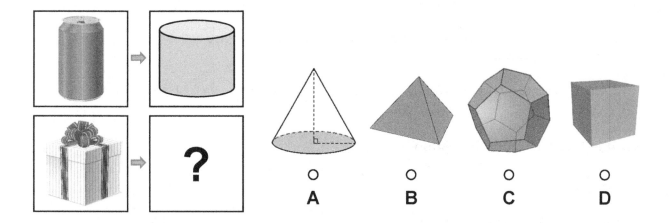

Verbal Analogies Drills Answers

Thought Exercise Answers
(Answers are samples only. Your answer, if different, may still be correct.)

1. Paw; *Explanation:* Hair belongs on humans and fur belongs on animals. Hands belong on humans and paws belong on animals.

2. Water; *Explanation:* A car travels on a road, and a boat travels on water. Other suggested answers are: lake, sea, and ocean.

3. Doll; *Explanation:* Pepsi is a brand of soda, and Barbie is a doll. Another suggested answer: toy.

4. Gallon; *Explanation:* There are four quarters in a dollar, just as there are four quarts in a gallon.

5. Feel; *Explanation:* Eating and tasting are both similar actions performed with the mouth, and touching and feeling are both similar actions performed by the hand or other body part.

6. Destroy; *Explanation:* Remember and forget are antonyms. Build and destroy are antonyms, too. Another suggested answers: break, take apart, and raze.

7. Dirty; *Explanation:* Clear water indicates that it is clean, while murky water indicates that it is dirty.

8. Round; *Explanation:* Bananas are long, so you could say that length is a shape characteristic of bananas. Oranges are round because they are spherical.

9. Coffee; *Explanation:* Both cake and pie are dessert items with similar shapes. Coffee and tea are both drinks derived from plants that help people to wake up or provide health benefits.

10. Egg; *Explanation:* The turkey is the representative food item of Thanksgiving, and the egg is the representative food item for Easter.

11. Staple; *Explanation:* Both a pen and marker are used for writing, and both a paper clip and staple hold papers together.

12. Go; *Explanation:* A red light or sign tells a driver to stop, while a green light tells a driver to go.

Example CogAT® Question Answer

Answer: **D**

Explanation: A can has a cylindrical shape. A gift box has a cubical shape.

Sentence Completion Guide

Overview

There are 18 sentence completion questions in the form 7, level 8 administration of the CogAT®. The student must completely fill in the bubble below the image he or she believes to be the correct answer.

Structure of the Sentence Completion Questions

In sentence completion questions, a question is asked in quotations, followed by the answer choices.

The questions are parsed in the form of, "Which one is …?" so that it is possible to answer each question by picking the correct image.

Tackling the Sentence Completion Questions

The first thing to do when solving a sentence completion question is to identify the key word or words of the question. That is, there should be one or two pivotal words that define

Further, because the question can be wholly answered by choosing a single image, each question is generally limited in what it can ask about.

Broadly speaking, the scope of the questions are limited to:

1. Purpose and Function
2. Categorization and Description
3. Characteristics and Traits

A purpose and function question may look like, "Which one is used for…" or "Which one can do…"

A categorization and description question may look like, "Which one belongs to…"

A characteristics and traits question may look like, "Which one looks…" or "Which one is similar to…"

In one sense, the sentence completion questions are the easiest, but in another sense they are not. They are the easiest in that they are the most direct. They are potentially the most difficult if the words that appear in the question are unfamiliar to the student; the student is at the mercy of the test writers.

Having your child read many books is one of the best ways to assure that your child's repertoire of vocabulary words remains robust.

What if the Answer is Not Obvious?

If it seems more than one image can be the answer to the question, it is important to look for the differences between the images. Sometimes, even small differences can be the difference between the correct answer and an incorrect one.

If your child does not know the key word(s) at all, then instead of instructing him or her to guess blindly, instruct him or her to see if he or she can find the image that is most dissimilar to the other images. Sometimes, even if the correct answer is not obvious, the most different answer can be the correct answer. That is, if the other choices all share some common similarity, but one doesn't, the odd choice out can be the correct answer. Of course, this is not a foolproof approach, but it certainly is one strategy to consider.

Sentence Completion Drills

Thought Exercises

Directions: Answer the following questions by circling the letter in front of the best answer choice.

1. "Which one is used for adding numbers quickly?"
   A. Ruler   B. Calculator   C. Compass   D. Chart

2. "Which one is not used for cleaning?"
   A. Dustpan   B. Mop   C. Thermos   D. Broom

3. "Which one is the scariest?"
   A. Deer   B. Flower   C. Panda   D. Ghost

4. "Which one is a carnivore?"
   A. Person   B. Cow   C. Tiger   D. Giraffe

5. "Which one has humps on its back?"
   A. Horse   B. Fox   C. Camel   D. Coyote

6. "Which one is usually found in a shopping mall?"
   A. Elevator   B. Bulldozer   C. Airplane   D. Ladder

7. "Which one is found in the South Pole?"
   A. Cheetah   B. Antelope   C. Duck   D. Penguin

8. "Which one gives directions?"
   A. Email   B. GPS   C. Radio   D. Headphone

Example CogAT® Question

Directions: Fill in the circle under the image that best answers the question.

"Which one is usually eaten for dessert at a friend's birthday party?"

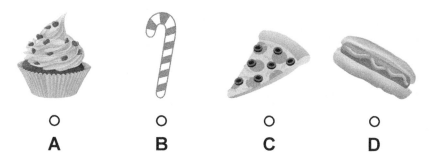

  A   B   C   D

Sentence Completion Drills Answers

Thought Exercise Answers

1. B, Calculator; *Explanation:* A ruler helps to measure, but not necessarily add. A compass helps to find direction, not add. A chart provides information, and some charts can help to figure out how to add numbers, but not all charts do. A calculator is the best answer here.

2. C, Thermos; *Explanation:* A thermos is a bottle used to hold various drinks and to keep them either cold or hot. The other answer choices are all used for cleaning.

3. D, Ghost; *Explanation:* The scariest thing on this list is the ghost, at least for most people. Deer, flowers, and pandas are not usually considered scary.

4. C, Tiger; *Explanation:* A carnivore is an animal that only feeds on meat. Tigers are the only carnivores in this list. People are omnivores, which are animals that eat both meat and plants. Cows and giraffes are herbivores, which are animals that eat only plants.

5. C, Camel; *Explanation:* The only animal in the list that has humps on its back is the camel.

6. A, Elevator; *Explanation:* Stairs, escalators, and elevators are the most common ways people are transported from one floor to another in a shopping mall. Since stairs and escalators aren't answer choices, the best answer is elevator.

7. D, Penguin; *Explanation:* Penguins are found in the southern hemisphere. And some penguin species are found in the South Pole (Antarctica). The other animals listed would probably not be able to survive in Antarctica, as they are probably not equipped for such extreme temperatures.

8. B, GPS; *Explanation:* The purpose of a GPS is to provide directions to a specified address or location in real time. While an email could be used to provide directions, that is not the sole function of emails. Thus, GPS is the best answer here.

Example CogAT® Question Answer

Answer: **A**

Explanation: A cupcake is considered a birthday dessert item. A candy cane is a holiday sweet, so it is not as good an answer. Pizzas and hot dogs, while often at birthday parties, are not considered desserts.

Verbal Classification Guide

Overview

There are 18 verbal classification questions in the form 7, level 8 administration of the CogAT®. The student must completely fill in the bubble below the image he or she believes to be the correct answer.

Structure of the Verbal Classification Questions

In verbal classification questions, there are 2 rows of images. The top row images make up the question. The bottom row is comprised of the answer choices and their images. The 2 rows are separated by line to reduce confusion. The outline of a question is shown in the figure below. Imagine that each square contains an image. Note that the actual questions will not necessarily contain the squares shown below.

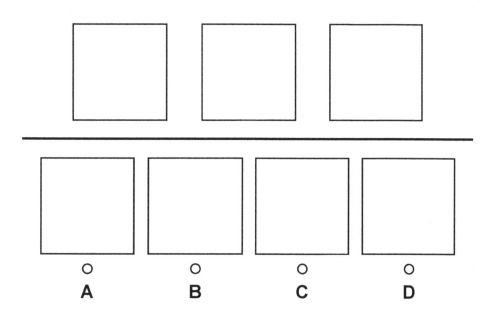

Tackling the Verbal Analogy Questions

The images in the top row are somehow alike in one way or another. The goal is to figure out which image among the answer choices belongs in the top row. Study the three images in the top row to find similarities between them.

Some similarities to take note of are:

1. Shape, Size, and Color
2. Use, Function, or Purpose
3. Object Classification
4. Characteristics and Traits

Find as many similarities as possible between the images of the top row. If there are, for instance, 2 similarities that all of the images in the top row share, then there is a great likelihood that the correct answer will share the same 2 similarities. The more specific the similarity, the better.

What if the Answer is Not Obvious?

If it seems more than one image can be the answer to the question, try counting the number of similarities there are between each of the answer choices and the images in the top row. The image with the most number of similarities will probably be the correct answer.

Verbal Classification Drills

Thought Exercises

Directions: Answer each of the following questions by circling the word that **least** belongs in the group of words.

1.	Red	Green	Yellow	Violet	Brown
2.	Flea	Cricket	Spider	Moth	Mosquito
3.	Desk	Tripod	Lens	Flash	Camera
4.	Watermelon	Coconut	Grapefruit	Cabbage	Orange
5.	Skeleton	Bone	Skull	Skin	Fossil
6.	Inch	Time	Yard	Foot	Meter
7.	Yummy	Tasty	Gross	Yucky	Bumpy
8.	Short	Long	Sticky	Wide	Tall
9.	Ripped	New	Rusty	Creaky	Torn
10.	Drill	Swing	Yo-yo	Jump rope	Trampoline

Example CogAT® Question

Directions: Answer the following question by filling in the bubble below the image that most belongs with the images in the top row.

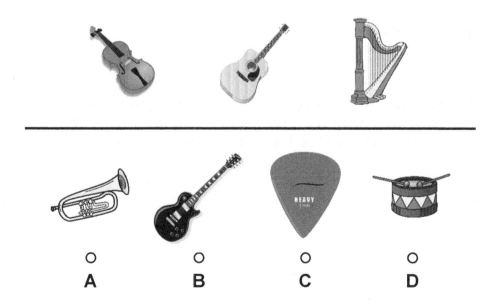

    A   B   C   D

Verbal Classification Drills Answers

Thought Exercise Answers

1. Brown; *Explanation:* Red, green, yellow, and violet are thought to be standard colors of the rainbow, whereas brown is not.

2. Spider; *Explanation:* Spider is the only animal that is not an insect. Spiders, with their 8 legs, are arachnids.

3. Desk; *Explanation:* Tripod, lens, flash, and camera are all words related to the process of using a camera to take a photograph. A desk is not related to the process of taking a photograph.

4. Cabbage; *Explanation:* In this list, cabbage is the only word that doesn't refer to a fruit.

5. Skin; *Explanation:* All of the other words have to do with bones, so skin, which doesn't directly relate to bones, least belongs in the group.

6. Time; *Explanation:* All of the other words have to do with length measurement units; time is the only word that is not a length measurement unit.

7. Bumpy; *Explanation:* Yummy, tasty, gross, and yucky all describe how good or bad a food's flavor is. Bumpy does not describe flavor.

8. Sticky; *Explanation:* The other words describe length or size, but sticky doesn't.

9. New; *Explanation:* Ripped, rusty, creaky, and torn all indicate less than perfection condition in some way. New, however, implies pristine and perfect.

10. Drill; *Explanation:* Everything else in the list refers to things that children play with or amuse themselves with. A drill is a tool used for construction or assembly, so it is not a toy.

Example CogAT® Question Answer

Answer: **B**

Explanation: The top row shows strings instruments, so the correct answer is the guitar, which is the only string instrument in the bottom row. A trumpet is a brass instrument, a guitar pick isn't an instrument in and of itself, and drums are percussion instruments.

Number Analogies Guide

Overview

There are 18 number analogies questions in the form 7, level 8 administration of the CogAT®. The student must completely fill in the bubble below the image he or she believes to be the correct answer.

Structure of the Number Analogies Questions

In number analogies questions, there are 4 squares, arranged in a 2-by-2 grid formation— that is, two squares on top and two squares on bottom. The answer choices will either be to the right or bottom of this 2-by-2 grid. The outline of a question is shown in the figure below.

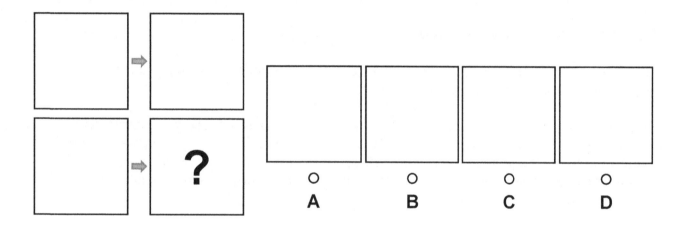

The numbers of objects or images in the top two squares are numerically related or correlated, so the numbers of objects or images in the bottom two squares are also related to each other in a similar way.

The bottom right square contains a question mark. The goal of the question is to figure out which answer choice replaces the question mark.

Tackling the Number Analogies Questions

To figure out which answer choice should replace the question mark, it is important to understand the number relationship between the images in the top two squares of each problem.

Study the top two squares in the grid and count the number of objects in the first square. Then count the number of objects in the second square and see how they might be related. The types of objects or images can be different. It's important to focus mostly on the numbers.

Ask the following question: How much needs to be added or subtracted from the top left square to get the number of objects or images found in the top right square?

Compare the answer choices to the bottom left square. If none of the answer choices seems to work, then think about either multiplying or dividing, as needed.

What if the Answer is Not Obvious?

If the answer is still not apparent, it is possible that a combination of multiplication or division and addition or subtraction is needed.

Furthermore, it may be possible that the correct answer does not follow the same pattern, but the inverse pattern, as long as the difference in the number of objects in the answer and the number of objects in the bottom left square is the same as the difference in the numbers of objects in the top two squares. *Only use this approach when positive that all other approaches are incorrect.*

Number Analogies Drills

Thought Exercises
Directions: For each question, circle the answer choice that best completes the number analogy.

1. Six is to Seven as Nine is to _____.
   A. Ten   B. Nine   C. Eleven   D. Eight

2. Four is to Six as Two is to _____.
   A. Zero   B. One   C. Two   D. Three

3. Nine is to Three as Twelve is to _____.
   A. Seven   B. Five   C. Six   D. Eight

4. Four is to Fourteen as One is to _____.
   A. Seven   B. Eight   C. Nine   D. Eleven

5. Sixteen is to Seven as Thirteen is to _____.
   A. Four   B. Five   C. Three   D. Two

6. One is to Two as Three is to _____.
   A. One   B. Two   C. Five   D. Six

7. Ten is to Seven as Five is to _____.
   A. Three   B. Two   C. Eight   D. Ten

8. Eight is to Five as Twelve is to _____.
   A. Five   B. Seven   C. Eleven   D. Thirteen

Example CogAT® Question
Directions: Fill in the circle below the answer choice of the image that best completes the analogy.

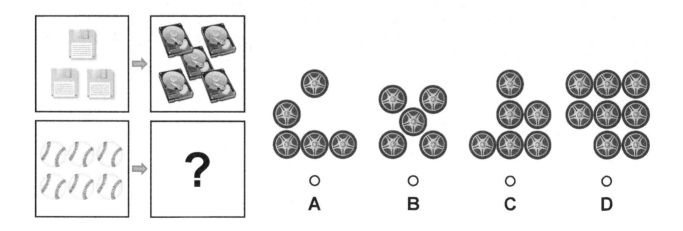

Number Analogies Drills Answers

Thought Exercise Answers

1. A, Ten; *Explanation:* 6 **+ 1** = 7, and 9 **+ 1** = 10.

2. D, Three; *Explanation:* 4 **× 1.5** = 6 (or 4 + 2 = 6), and 2 **× 1.5** = 3 (or 2 + 1 = 3). Since most 2nd grade students do not have the concept of multiplication, and especially not with decimals, one way to explain this concept is to teach it to them by grouping. For this problem, splitting 4 into 2 groups leads to 2 groups of 2. If the quantity of one of the groups is added back to 4, then the result is 6. Similarly, if 2 is split into 2 groups, we get 2 groups of 1. Then 2 + 1 = 3. It might help to demonstrate using real objects, if your child is having difficulty understanding the concept abstractly.

3. C, Six; *Explanation:* 9 **− 6** = 3, and 12 **− 6** = 6.

4. D, Eleven; *Explanation:* 4 **+ 10** = 14, and 1 **+ 10** = 11.

5. A, Four; *Explanation:* 16 **− 9** = 7, and 13 **− 9** = 4.

6. D, Six; *Explanation:* 1 **× 2** = 2, and 3 **× 2** = 6. Note that the other choices don't work. 1 + 1 = 2, but there is no answer choice of 4, so it can't be 3 + 1 = 4. Thus, we can eliminate + 1 as the operation that needs to be performed.

7. B, Two; *Explanation:* 10 **− 3** = 7, and 5 **− 3** = 2.

8. B, Seven; *Explanation:* 8 **÷ 2 + 1** = 5, and 12 **÷ 2 + 1** = 7. Ordinarily, the answer should be 9, as 8 − 3 = 5, and 12 − 3 = 9. Nine is not an answer choice, however, so it is important to switch to another way of thinking about the relationship between 8 and 5. In other words, if 8 is divided into 2 groups, and 1 is added to one of the groups of 4, then 5 is the result. Similarly, split 12 into 2 groups of 6. Add 1 to one of the groups to get 6 + 1 = 7.

Example CogAT® Question Answer

Answer: **D**

Explanation: There are 3 floppy disks and 5 hard drives. There are two more hard drives than there are floppy disks. The relationship between the numbers is 3 + 2 = 5. There are 6 baseballs, so there should be 2 more wheels to maintain the same relationship. 6 + 2 = 8, so D is the correct answer.

Number Puzzles Guide

Overview

There are 14 number puzzles questions in the form 7, level 8 administration of the CogAT®. The student must completely fill in the bubble below the image he or she believes to be the correct answer.

Structure of the Number Puzzles Questions

In number puzzles questions, there are 2 trains separated by a vertical line. Each side of this line represents a side of a mathematical equation. Thus, both sides combined make up a full equation.

One of the trains (very likely to be the one on the left side of the vertical line) is depicted as carrying a certain number of cargo items. The other train on the other side of the vertical line has more cars (usually 2 in total) and a fewer number of cargo items—one of this train's cars contains the cargo items and the other contains a question mark. The outline of a number puzzle question is shown below.

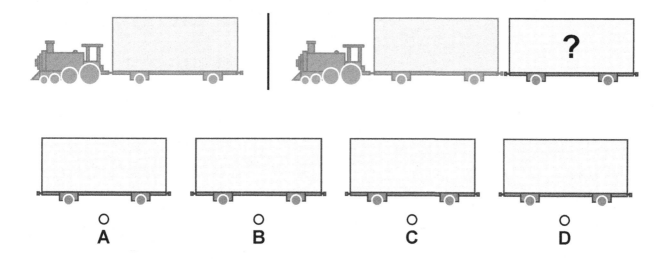

The goal is to determine which answer choice should replace the car containing the question mark by figuring out how many cargo items the mystery car should contain.

Tackling the Number Puzzles Questions

Think of number puzzles questions as addition or subtraction problems. To find the correct answer, determine how many more cargo objects must be added to the right train in order to make it carry the same number of cargo objects as the left train is carrying.

Count the number of items the left train is carrying and subtract that by the number of objects the right train is already carrying. This will give you the answer to how many objects the left train's mystery car should carry.

If the answer is not obvious at first, then try recounting the number of objects and making sure the subtraction or addition was done correctly.

Number Puzzles Drills

Thought Exercises

Directions: For each question, write in the correct answer to satisfy the equation.

1. 3 = 2 + _____

2. 9 = 6 + _____

3. 10 = 4 + _____

4. 15 = 8 + _____

5. 8 + _____ = 11

6. 5 + _____ = 14

7. 13 + _____ = 18

8. 7 + _____ = 19

9. _____ + 7 = 11

10. _____ + 9 = 9

11. _____ + 5 = 13

12. _____ + 10 = 20

13. 13 = 2 + 4 + _____

14. 17 = 4 + 11 + _____

15. 13 + _____ + 3 = 21

16. 0 + _____ + 14 = 20

17. _____ + 4 + 8 = 13

18. _____ + 4 + 4 = 19

Example CogAT® Question

Directions: Choose the answer choice that is needed to give the second train the same number of objects as the first train.

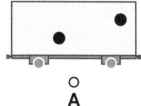 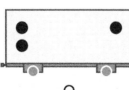  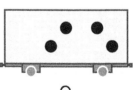

A   B   C   D

Number Puzzles Drills Answers

Thought Exercise Answers

1. 1; *Explanation:* 3 = 2 + 1.

2. 3; *Explanation:* 9 = 6 + 3.

3. 6; *Explanation:* 10 = 4 + 6.

4. 7; *Explanation:* 15 = 8 + 7.

5. 3; *Explanation:* 8 + 3 = 11.

6. 9; *Explanation:* 5 + 9 = 14.

7. 5; *Explanation:* 13 + 5 = 18.

8. 12; *Explanation:* 7 + 12 = 19.

9. 4; *Explanation:* 4 + 7 = 11.

10. 0; *Explanation:* 0 + 9 = 9.

11. 8; *Explanation:* 8 + 5 = 13.

12. 10; *Explanation:* 10 + 10 = 20.

13. 7; *Explanation:* 13 = 2 + 4 + 7.

14. 2; *Explanation:* 17 = 4 + 11 + 2.

15. 5; *Explanation:* 13 + 5 + 3 = 21.

16. 6; *Explanation:* 0 + 6 + 14 = 20.

17. 1; *Explanation:* 1 + 4 + 8 = 13.

18. 11; *Explanation:* 11 + 4 + 4 = 19.

Example CogAT® Question Answer

Answer: **D**

Explanation: The left train is carrying 5 objects. The first car of the right train is carrying 1. This means that the second car of the right train must be carrying 4 objects, since 5 = 1 + 4 or 5 − 1 = 4.

Number Series Guide

Overview

There are 18 number series questions in the form 7, level 8 administration of the CogAT®. The student must completely fill in the bubble below the image he or she believes to be the correct answer.

Structure of the Number Series Questions

In number series questions, there is an abacus that contains columns of beads or circles. A sample question template is shown below. (On the actual test, the answer choices may be to the right of the abacus.)

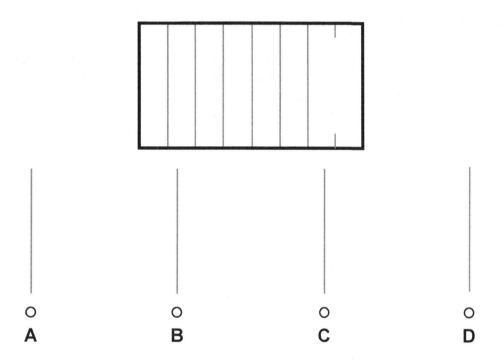

The last column of beads is missing beads, so the goal is to find the correct number of beads that should occupy that column.

Tackling the Number Series Questions

Number series questions can be answered by finding the pattern of the number of beads. Count the number of beads in the columns. Then compare the numbers of beads in the columns.

Look for some of the following common patterns for the numbers of beads:

1. Straight pattern: the number of beads increases or decreases by a set amount with each column move to the right.
2. Leapfrog pattern: the number of beads increases or decreases by a set amount every other column, while the other columns retain the same number.
3. Alternating patterns: two patterns exist concurrently in an alternating fashion, such that the odd numbered columns adhere to one pattern while the even numbered columns adhere to another.

What if the Answer is Not Obvious?

If the answer is still not apparent, try to think outside the box. Look for other patterns that do not necessarily conform to the common patterns listed above. Work through the thought exercises on the next page to get a better feel for the more "unorthodox" problems.

Number Series Drills

Thought Exercises

Directions: Given the numbers, find the next number in the pattern.

1. 6, 5, 4, 3, 2, 1, _____ .

2. 3, 6, 9, 12, 15, 18, _____ .

3. 10, 15, 20, 25, 30, 35, _____ .

4. 1, 5, 7, 5, 13, 5, _____ .

5. 7, 8, 10, 13, 17, 22, _____ .

6. 27, 23, 19, 15, 11, 7, _____ .

7. 9, 11, 7, 9, 11, 7, _____ .

8. 8, 8, 15, 15, 22, 22, _____ .

9. 0, 2, 2, 4, 8, 16, _____ .

10. 1, 8, 3, 6, 9, 4, _____ .

Example CogAT® Question

Directions: Fill in the circle below the column of beads that would appear next in the series.

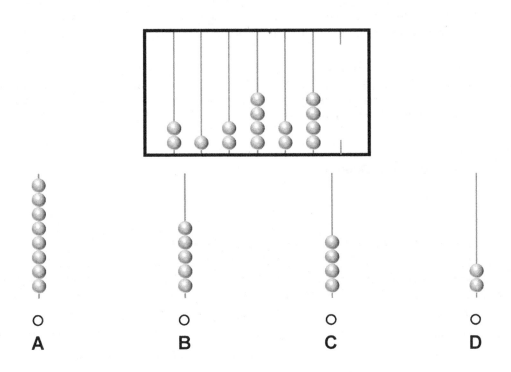

Number Series Drills Answers

Thought Exercise Answers

1. 0; *Explanation:* The numbers decrease by 1. 1 – 1 = 0.

2. 21; *Explanation:* The numbers increase by 3. 18 + 3 = 21.

3. 40; *Explanation:* The numbers increase by 5. 35 + 5 = 40.

4. 19; *Explanation:* The odd numbered terms increase by 6, while the even numbered terms stay constant at 5. The 7th term is 13 + 6 = 19.

5. 28; *Explanation:* The differences between the terms increases by 1 each time. The difference between 7 and 8 is 1. The difference between 8 and 10 is 2. The difference 10 and 13 is 3. The difference between 13 and 17 is 4. The difference between 17 and 22 is 5. The difference between 22 and the next term should be 6, then. 22 + 6 = 28.

6. 3; *Explanation:* The numbers decrease by 4. 7 – 4 = 3.

7. 9; *Explanation:* The numbers 9, 11, and 7 repeat in a cycle. Since the 6th number ended with a 7, the cycle of 9, 11, and 7 will start again. The next number after 7 is 9.

8. 29; *Explanation:* Each number is repeated twice, starting at 8. The next number after 15, which is repeated twice, is 22. That means that the difference between pairs of numbers is 7: 8 + 7 = 15, and 15 + 7 = 22, so 22 + 7 = 29.

9. 32; *Explanation:* Starting with the third number, each number is the sum of all the numbers before it. For instance, 0 + 2 = 2, which is the third number. The fourth number is 0 + 2 + 2 = 4, the fifth number is 0 + 2 + 2 + 4 = 8, and the sixth number is 0 + 2 + 2 + 4 + 8 = 16, so the seventh number is 0 + 2 + 2 + 4 + 8 + 16 = 32. Another approach: starting with the 4th number, each number is twice the previous number, or, in other words, each number is the previous number added to itself.

10. 27; *Explanation:* The odd-numbered terms are multiples of 3, starting with the second odd-numbered term: 1 x 3 = 3, 3 x 3 = 9, so 9 x 3 = 27. If your child does not know how to multiply yet, teach them to add the same number by itself three times: 1 + 1 + 1 = 3, 3 + 3 + 3 = 9, so 9 + 9 + 9 = 27. The even-numbered terms decrease by 2: 8 – 2 = 6, 6 – 2 = 4.

Example CogAT® Question Answer

Answer: **A**

Explanation: The numbers of beads in the abacus can be expressed as 2, 1, 2, 4, 2, 4. Notice the numbers can be broken up into two groups: 2, 1, 2 and 4, 2, 4. Each number in the 2nd set is twice each of the corresponding numbers in the 1st set. The next set of numbers would likely be 8, 4, 8, so 8 would be the 7th number and therefore the correct answer. Note: A student may think (justifiably so) that the 1st and 3rd numbers of the 2nd set are 2 bigger than those of the first set, meaning the 1st and 3rd numbers of the next set are 6 (4 + 2). 6 beads is not an option, however, so this approach is incorrect.

Figure Matrices Guide

Overview

There are 18 figure matrices questions in the form 7, level 8 administration of the CogAT®. The student must completely fill in the bubble below the image he or she believes to be the correct answer.

Structure of the Figure Matrices Questions

In figure matrices questions, there are 4 squares, arranged in a 2-by-2 grid formation—that is, two squares on top and two squares on bottom. The answer choices will either be to the right or bottom of this 2-by-2 grid. The outline of a question is shown in the figure below.

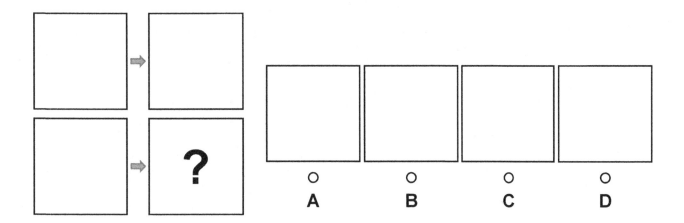

The figures or shapes in the top two squares are related or correlated in some way, so the numbers of objects or images in the bottom two squares are also related to each other in a similar way.

The bottom right square contains a question mark. The goal of the question is to figure out which answer choice replaces the question mark.

Tackling the Figure Matrices Questions

In solving figure matrices questions, look for the relationships and similarities between the shapes or figures in the top squares of the question. Some of the relationships and similarities to look for are:

1. Shape and Number of Sides
2. Arrangement of Figures
3. Color and Shading
4. Size
5. Rotations

Figure Matrices Drills

Thought Exercises

Directions: For each question, a figure is provided to the right of the question. Redraw the figure according to all three of the conditions stated.

1. A. Size of Side Lengths: 1x (Same)
   B. Color and Shading: Black
   C. Rotation: 45°

2. A. Size of Dimensions: 1x (Same)
   B. Color and Shading: Gray
   C. Rotation: 90° Clockwise

3. A. Size of Dimensions: 0.5x (Half)
   B. Color and Shading: No Change
   C. Rotation: 90° Counterclockwise

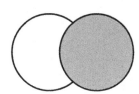

4. A. Size of Side Lengths: 1x (Same)
   B. Color and Shading: No Change
   C. Rotation: 180°

5. A. Size of Side Lengths: 2x (Double)
   B. Color and Shading: Inverted (Flipped)
   C. Rotation: 180°

Example CogAT® Question

Directions: Choose the answer choice that best completes the analogy.

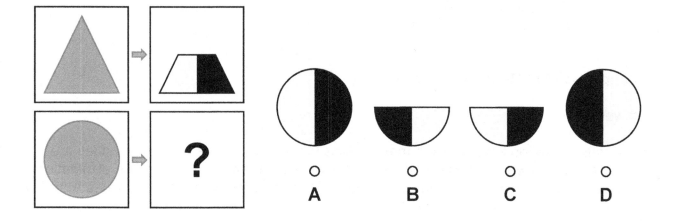

37

Number Puzzles Drills Answers

Thought Exercise Answers

1.

Explanation: The side lengths of the figure above are the same size of the original's on the previous page. The figure has been shaded black and rotated 45°. (For this exercise, it doesn't matter whether the figure was rotated clockwise or counterclockwise.)

2.

Explanation: The dimensions of the three-quarters circle above are the same as the original's on the previous page. The figure has also been shaded gray. It has been rotated 90° clockwise.

3.

Explanation: The dimensions of the figure are half the original's on the previous page. The figure's shading has not been changed. The triangle has also been rotated 180° (or a full upside-down flip).

4.

Explanation: The dimensions of the figure above are the same size as the original's on the previous page. The figure's shading has not been changed. It has been rotated 180°. (It doesn't matter whether the figure was rotated clockwise or counterclockwise.)

5.

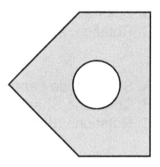

Explanation: The side lengths of the figure above are double the size of the original's on the previous page. The figure's shading has also been flipped. It has been rotated 180°.

Example CogAT® Question Answer

Answer: **C**

Explanation: The top left figure is a triangle. The top right is a trapezoid whose sides are shaded black and white. The relationship may not be clear at this point, so use elimination to answer this question The triangle and trapezoid are different shapes, so choices A and D should be eliminated, as both are still just full circles. Then eliminate B because the shading pattern is flipped. Also, another way to think about the relationship between the triangle and trapezoid is that the trapezoid is the triangle with the top cut off.

Paper Folding Guide

Overview

There are 14 paper folding questions in the form 7, level 8 administration of the CogAT®. The student must completely fill in the bubble below the image he or she believes to be the correct answer.

Structure of the Paper Folding Questions

Paper folding questions start with a diagram of a square sheet of paper. This square is folded once or more, either horizontally, vertically, or diagonally. After the paper is finished being folded, one or more holes are punched into the paper. The purpose of paper folding questions is to figure out how many holes the square sheet of paper will have when it is fully unfolded.

Below are the ways that a paper can be single-folded:

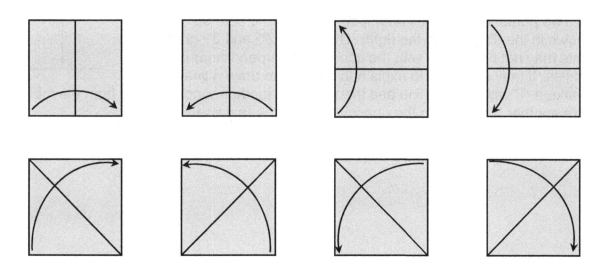

After the first fold, you may see a second fold on the test. Below are some of the ways a second fold can happen:

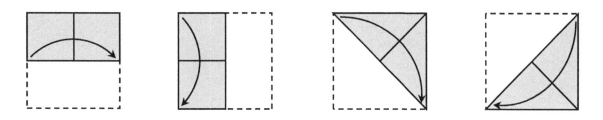

Tackling the Paper Folding Questions

In solving paper folding questions, it is important to be able to understand and identify the lines of symmetry for the folding. Luckily, the fold lines are the lines of symmetry.

The first key to solving paper folding questions is realizing that each time the paper is unfolded, the number of holes in the paper is double the number of holes that were in the paper before the paper is unfolded.

The second key to solving paper folding questions is realizing that the second set of holes is a mirror reflection of the first set of holes but across the fold line. This means that the two sets of holes are directly opposite from each other across the fold line. Furthermore, the corresponding holes are equidistant from the fold line.

Tip: Starting from the center of each hole, draw a line perpendicular* to the fold line. For each perpendicular line you drew, draw a line of equal length and opposite direction from the fold line. You will now have the locations of all of the circles' centers. Draw the circles around their centers, and you will have the image of the paper as it should look after the holes are punched.

*Note: Two perpendicular lines intersect, or meet, to create 90° angles (as shown in the diagram on the right). Of course, 2nd and 3rd grade students may not be familiar with the concept of perpendicular lines and 90° angles. It may be easier to explain to children to draw a line until they make a 'T' with the fold line and then to draw another congruent line from the fold line to make another 'T' that is on the opposite side of the fold line.

Paper Folding Drills

Thought Exercises

Directions: For each question, draw the mirror image of the shape or figure across fold line.

1.

2.

3.

4.

5.

6.

7.

8.

Example CogAT® Question

Directions: Fill in the circle below the image of the paper as it would look unfolded all the way.

A

B

C

D

Paper Folding Drills Answers

Thought Exercise Answers

Explanation: Draw a perpendicular line from each vertex (or center, if it's a circle) of the figure to the fold line. Then, for each line drawn to the fold line, draw a congruent perpendicular line from the fold line to the other side of the fold line. Then connect the vertices, or draw a circle, to create the mirror image (shown here in dotted lines).

1.

5.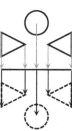

2.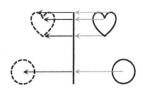

6.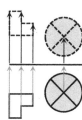

3.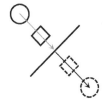

7.

4.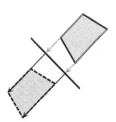

8.

Example CogAT® Question Answer

Answer: **B**

Explanation: Using the perpendicular line method described in guide, we see that after unfolding the paper once, there should be 8 holes:

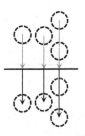

Use the perpendicular line method again, but this time for all 8 holes and vertically. This will lead to 8 more holes, for a total of 16 holes, in the configuration of the correct answer.

Figure Classification Guide

Overview

There are 18 figure classification questions in the form 7, level 8 administration of the CogAT®. The student must completely fill in the bubble below the image he or she believes to be the correct answer.

Structure of the Figure Classification Questions

In figure classification questions, there are 2 sets of images. The sets are separated by a dividing line to reduce confusion. The images in the first set comprise the question and the images in the second set comprise the answer choices.

In this book, each question has been arranged into 2 rows, with the top set comprising the question and the bottom set comprising the answer choices. An outline of a question has been provided below to show the structure of how the questions are formatted in this book.

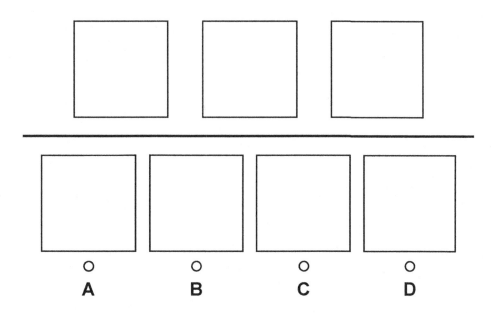

On the actual test itself, the question set and the answer choice set may be all arranged on the same row, with the question set to the left of the dividing line and the answer choice set to the line's right.

Regardless of the layout of the questions, the logic behind the questions is all the same. The images in the question set are all related in some way. That is, they are all similar in at least one way.

Tackling the Figure Classification Questions

In solving figure classification questions, take note of:

1. Shape
2. Size
3. Color or Shading
4. Patterns

Find as many similarities as possible between the images of the question set. If there are, for instance, 2 similarities that all of the images in the top row share, then there is a great likelihood that the correct answer will share the same 2 similarities. The more specific the similarity or similarities, the better.

What if the Answer is Not Obvious?

If it seems more than one image can be the answer to the question, try counting the number of similarities there are between each of the answer choices and the images in the top row. The image with the most number of similarities will probably be the correct answer.

Figure Classification Drills

Thought Exercises

Directions: For each question, draw a circle around the figure that **least** belongs in the group.

1.

2.

3.

4.

5.

6.

7.

8.

9.

10.

11.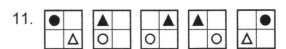

12.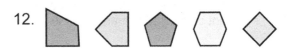

Example CogAT® Question

Directions: Fill in the circle below the image of figure that belongs in the top row.

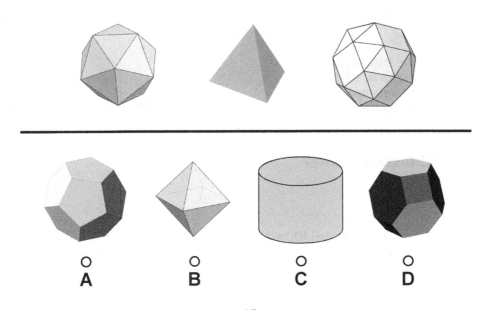

A   B   C   D

Figure Classification Drills Answers

Thought Exercise Answers

1.

   Explanation: This is the only arrow with a different shading pattern.

2.

   Explanation: This is the only figure whose interior figure is not a polygon of some sort.

3.

   Explanation: This is the only figure without diagonal shading.

4.

   Explanation: This is the only figure that is not composed of triangles of any sort.

5.

   Explanation: This is the only figure whose arrow is not pointing left or right.

6.

   Explanation: This is the only figure whose inner figure has the same shading positioning as the larger figure (white on white and gray on gray).

7.

   Explanation: This is the only figure that has pointed or sharp vertices.

8.

   Explanation: This is the only figure that doesn't have any concavity (indentations or dips in the sides).

9.

   Explanation: This is the only figure that doesn't have a black border and center.

10.

    Explanation: This is the only figure whose two figures overlap in opposite orientations.

11.

    Explanation: This is the only figure that has a triangle and circle on the same side of the grid.

12.

    Explanation: This is the only figure that does not have any lines of symmetry.

Example CogAT® Question Answer

Answer: **B**

Explanation: In each of figures in the top row, the figures are all 3-D shapes that have at least one triangle face. The figure in (B) is the only one that also has at least one triangle face.

PRACTICE
Test

VERBAL
Battery

VERBAL
ANALOGIES

DIRECTIONS & EXAMPLE QUESTION

The following directions are to be used for all verbal analogies questions:

Directions: For each question, in the grid of 4 squares, the top two figures are related in some way. Choose the answer choice that goes with the bottom left figure in a similar way.

Below is an example verbal analogies question:

Explanation: A plane is a vehicle that flies and eagle is an animal that flies. A sailboat is a vehicle that travels in water. None of the answer choices fits perfectly, as none of the animals are completely aquatic. But of the answer choices, A works the best because beavers by nature spend a significant time in and around water.

Question 1

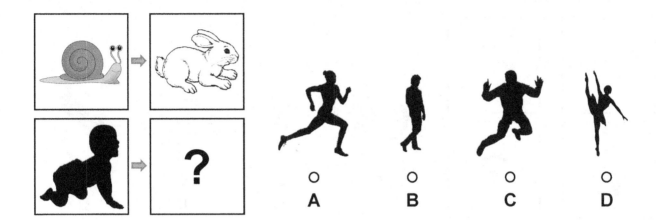

Question 2

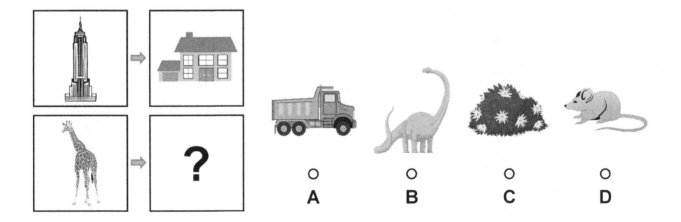

Question 3

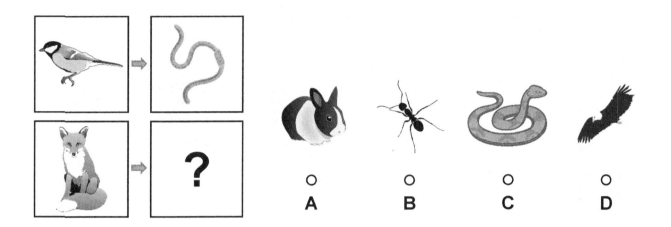

O   O   O   O
A   B   C   D

Question 4

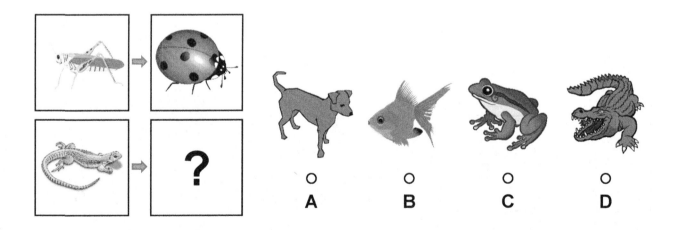

O   O   O   O
A   B   C   D

Question 5

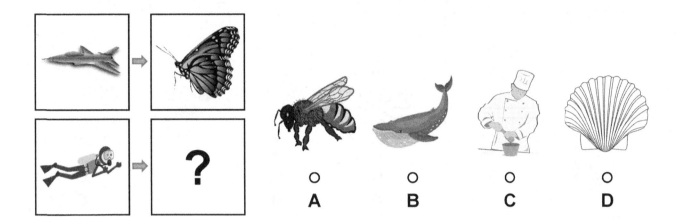

A B C D

Question 6

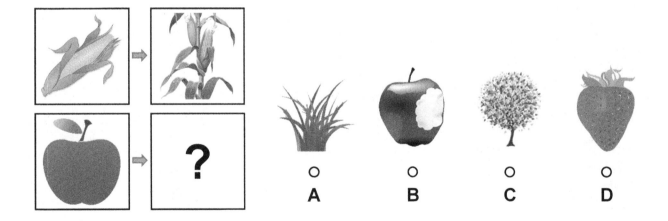

A B C D

Question 7

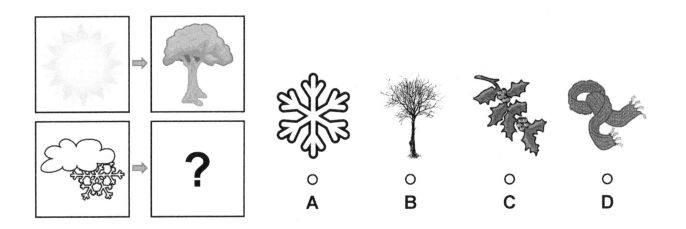

A   B   C   D

Question 8

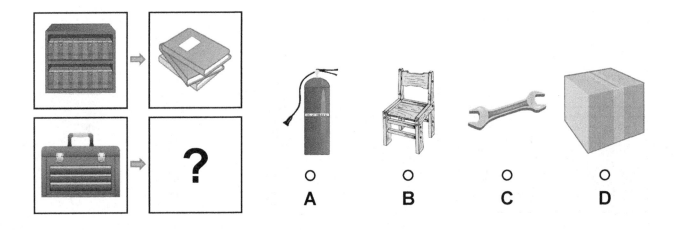

A   B   C   D

Question 9

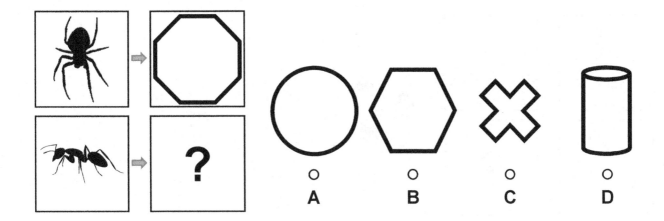

Question 10

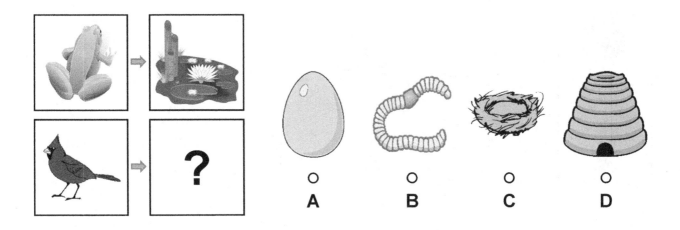

Question 11

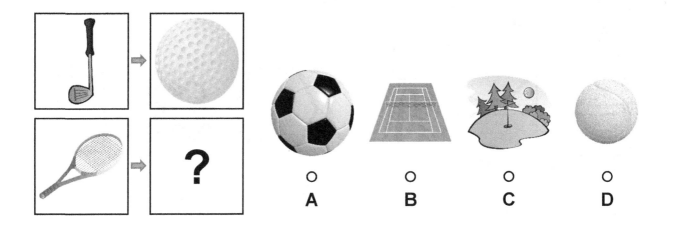

Question 12

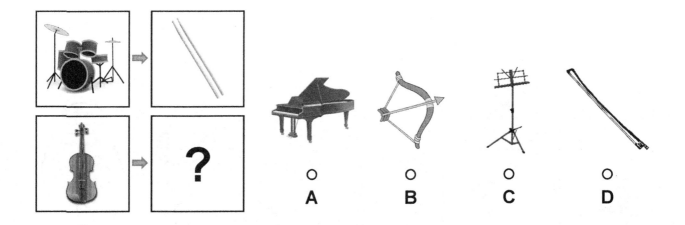

Question 13

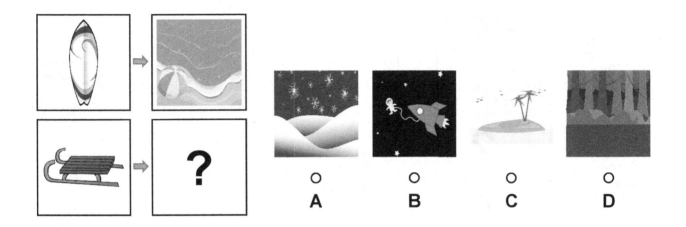

A   B   C   D

Question 14

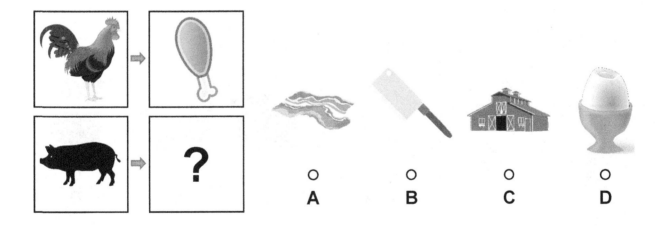

A   B   C   D

Question 15

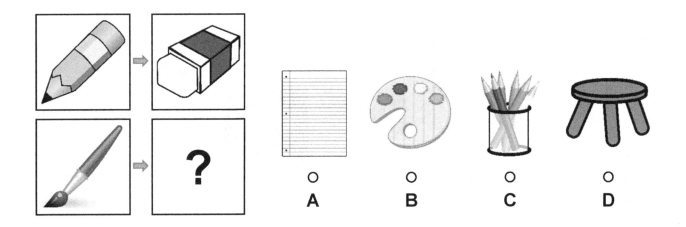

Question 16

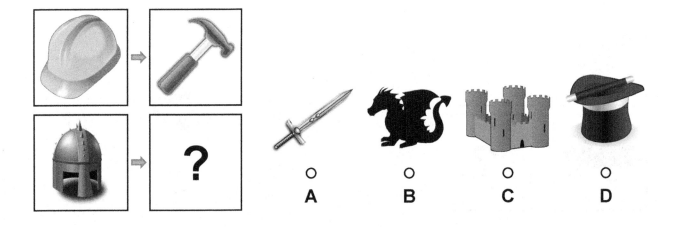

Question 17

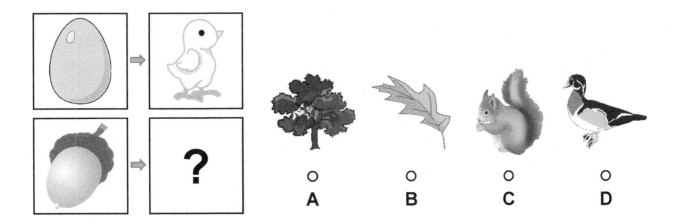

A B C D

Question 18

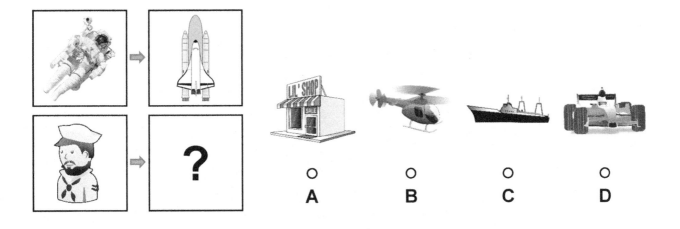

A B C D

SENTENCE
COMPLETION

Directions & Example Question

The following directions are to be used for all sentence completion questions:

Directions: Choose the answer choice that best answers the question presented.

Below is an example sentence completion question:

Example Question

"Which one is a ride at an amusement park?"

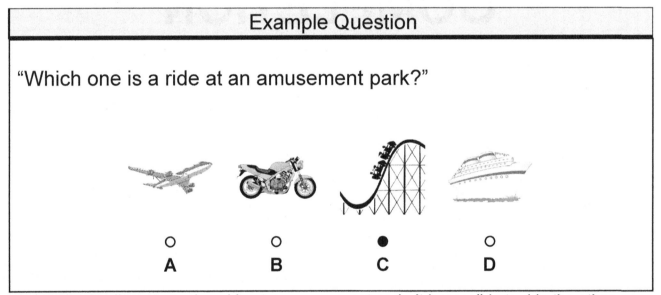

○	○	●	○
A	**B**	**C**	**D**

Example: A roller coaster is a ride at an amusement park. It is possible to ride the other objects shown, but they are not rides in an amusement park.

Question 1

"Which one has wings?"

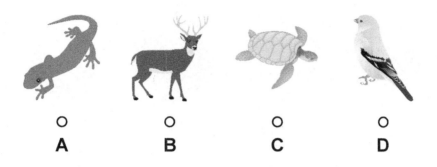

A   B   C   D

Question 2

"Which one is used for drawing?"

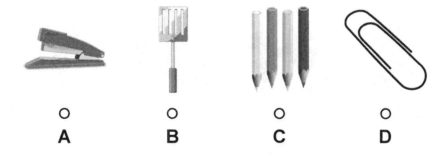

A   B   C   D

Question 3

"Which one can be found in a classroom?"

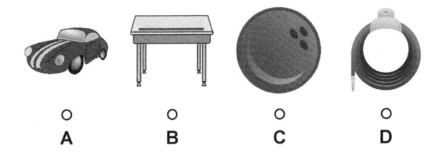

O	O	O	O
A	**B**	**C**	**D**

Question 4

"Which one is the heaviest?"

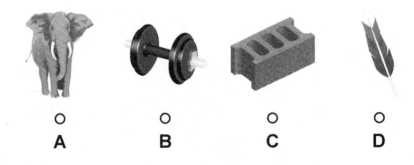

O	O	O	O
A	**B**	**C**	**D**

Question 5

"Which one is not used for cooking?"

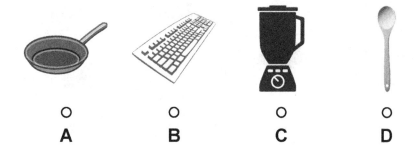

A	B	C	D
○	○	○	○

Question 6

"Which one lives in the desert?"

A	B	C	D
○	○	○	○

Question 7

"Which one is the tallest?"

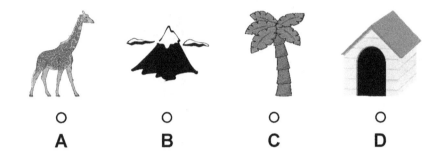

    ○   ○   ○   ○
    A   B   C   D

Question 8

"Which one is used for exercising?"

    ○   ○   ○   ○
    A   B   C   D

Question 9

"Which one has claws?"

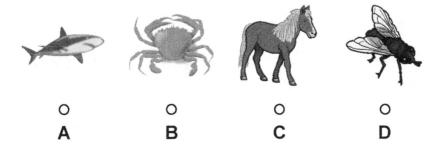

A   B   C   D

Question 10

"Which one drains water from food?"

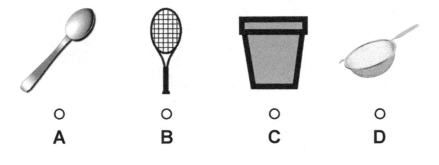

A   B   C   D

Question 11

"Which one is usually dessert at a friend's birthday party?"

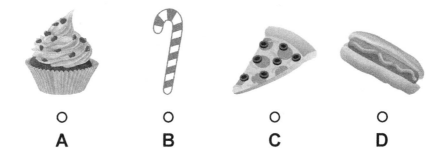

    ○   ○   ○   ○

    A   B   C   D

Question 12

"Which one is venomous?"

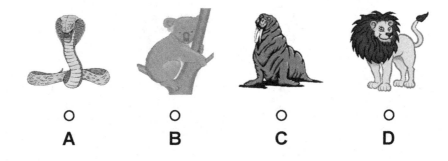

    ○   ○   ○   ○

    A   B   C   D

Question 13

"Which one is used for transportation?"

| A | B | C | D |

Question 14

"Which one is nocturnal?"

| A | B | C | D |

Question 15

"Which one is used for measuring length?"

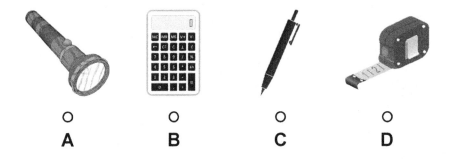

     O   O   O   O

     A   B   C   D

Question 16

"Which one repairs broken things?"

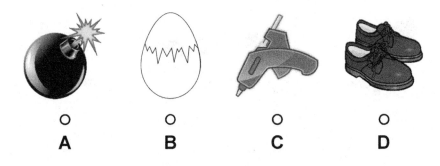

     O   O   O   O

     A   B   C   D

Question 17

"Which one can be found in the sky?"

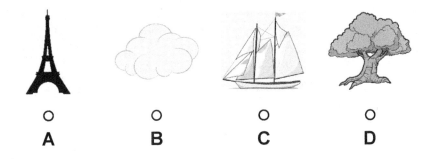

A	B	C	D
○	○	○	○
A	B	C	D

Question 18

"Which one is used for waking people up?"

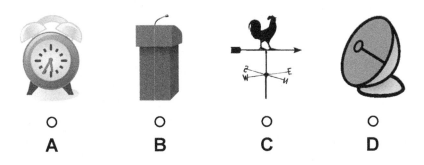

A	B	C	D
○	○	○	○
A	B	C	D

VERBAL
CLASSIFICATION

DIRECTIONS & EXAMPLE QUESTION

The following directions are to be used for all verbal classification questions:

Directions: The figures in the top row are alike in some way. Choose the figure in the bottom row that most belongs with the figures in the top row.

Below is an example verbal classification question:

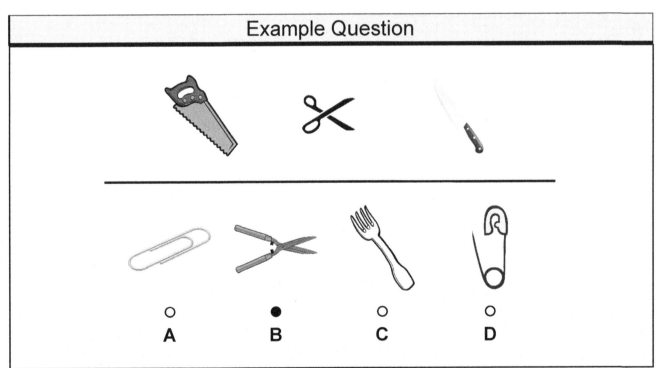

Example Question

○	●	○	○
A	B	C	D

Explanation: All of the figures in the top row are tools mainly used for cutting. Shears are also a tool used primarily for cutting, especially when gardening. Forks are not primarily used for cutting and neither are safety pins.

Question 1

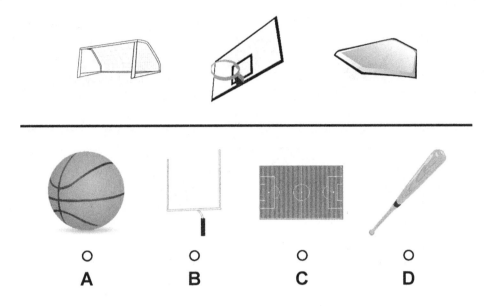

O
A

O
B

O
C

O
D

Question 2

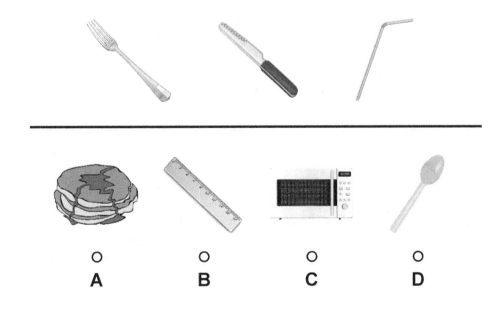

O
A

O
B

O
C

O
D

Question 3

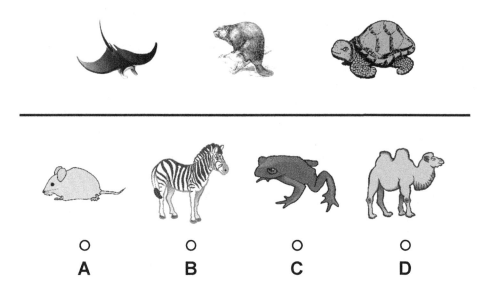

O	O	O	O
A	**B**	**C**	**D**

Question 4

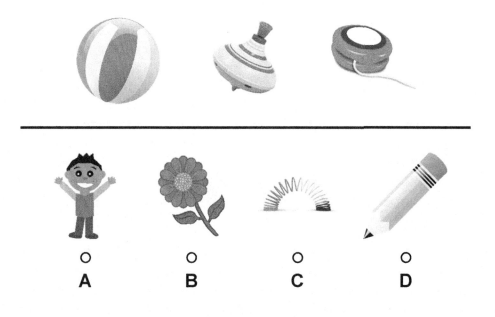

O	O	O	O
A	**B**	**C**	**D**

Question 5

○   ○   ○   ○

A   **B**   **C**   **D**

Question 6

○   ○   ○   ○

A   **B**   **C**   **D**

Question 7

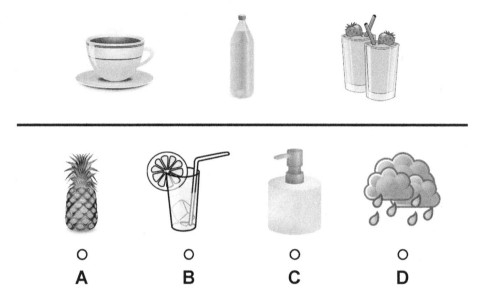

O
A

O
B

O
C

O
D

Question 8

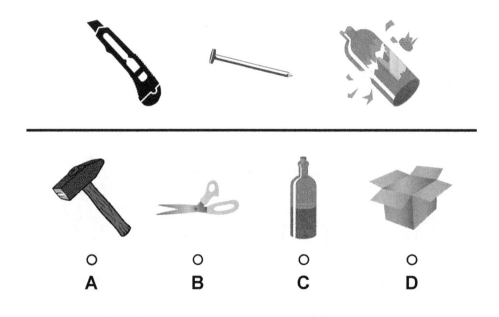

O
A

O
B

O
C

O
D

Question 9

○   ○   ○   ○
A   **B**   **C**   **D**

Question 10

○   ○   ○   ○
A   **B**   **C**   **D**

Question 11

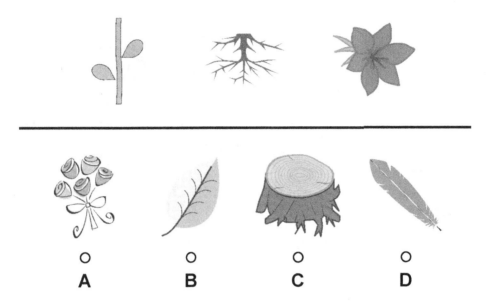

A B C D

Question 12

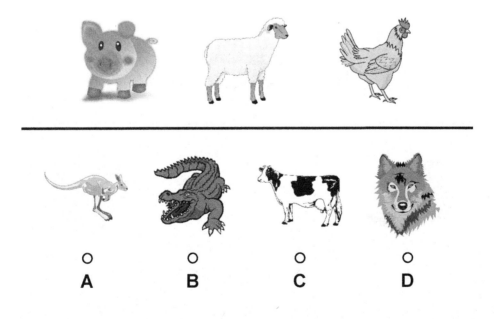

A B C D

Question 13

○   ○   ○   ○

A   **B**   **C**   **D**

Question 14

○   ○   ○   ○

A   **B**   **C**   **D**

Question 15

      O   O   O
A   B   C   D

Question 16

      O   O   O
A   B   C   D

Question 17

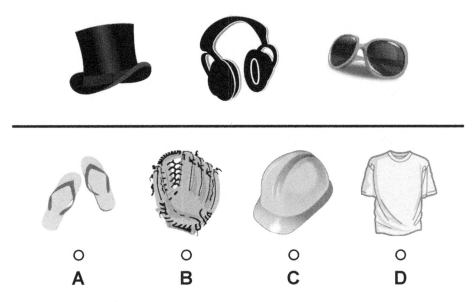

○ A ○ B ○ C ○ D

Question 18

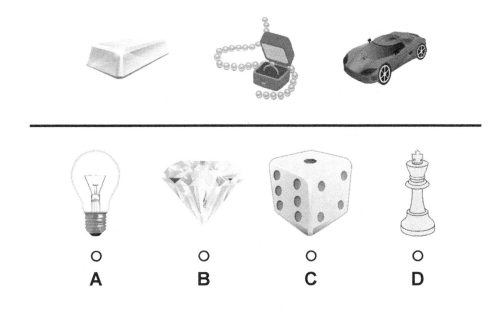

○ A ○ B ○ C ○ D

QUANTITATIVE
Battery

NUMBER
ANALOGIES

DIRECTIONS & EXAMPLE QUESTION

The following directions are to be used for all number analogies questions:

> **Directions:** For each question, in the grid of four squares, the top two figures are related to each other numerically. Choose the answer choice that is related to the bottom left figure in the same way numerically.

Below is an example number analogies question:

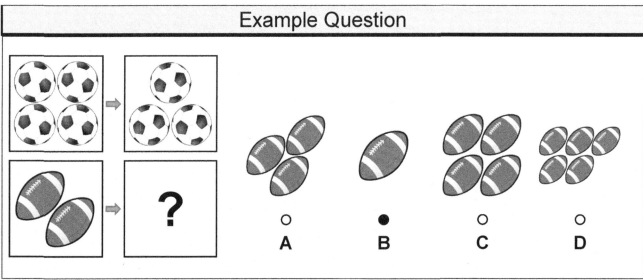

Example Question

Explanation: The first square contains 4 soccer balls. The second square contains 3, which is 1 fewer than 4. The correct answer is B because 1 fewer than 2 is 1. In other words, 2 – 1 = 1.

Question 1

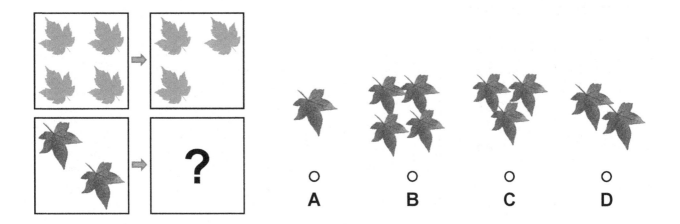

Question 2

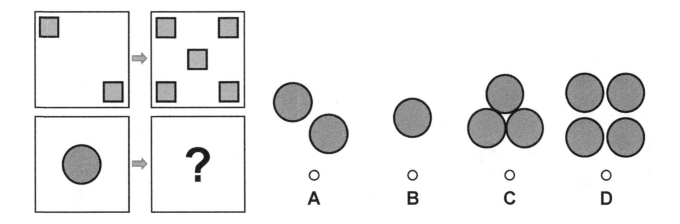

Question 3

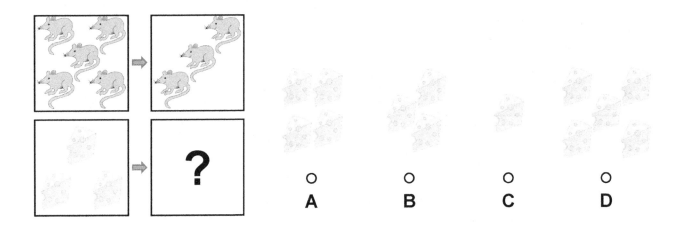

Question 4

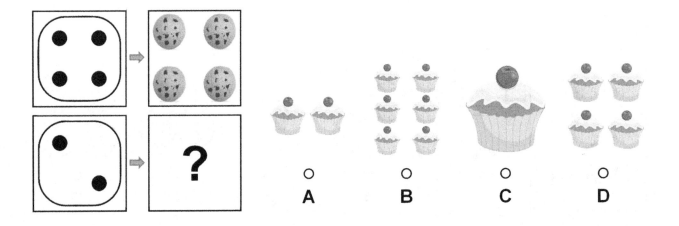

Question 5

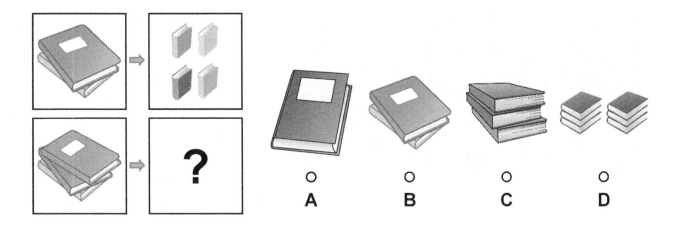

Question 6

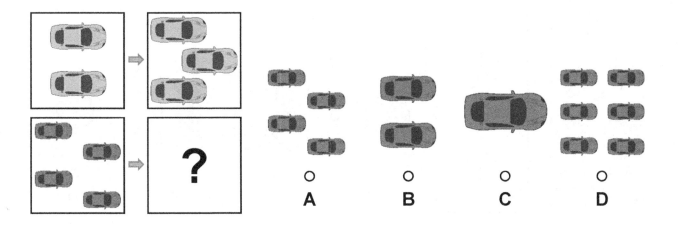

Question 7

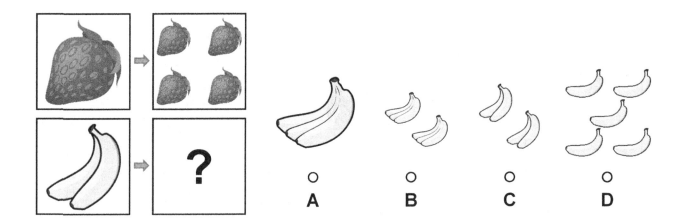

A   B   C   D

Question 8

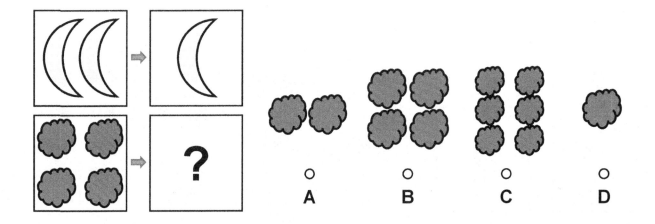

A   B   C   D

Question 9

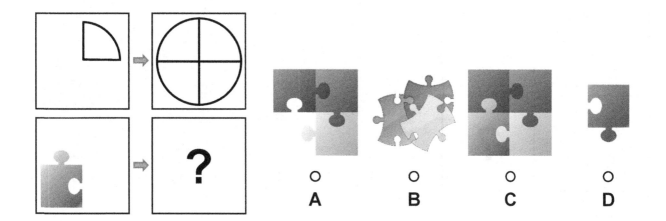

Question 10

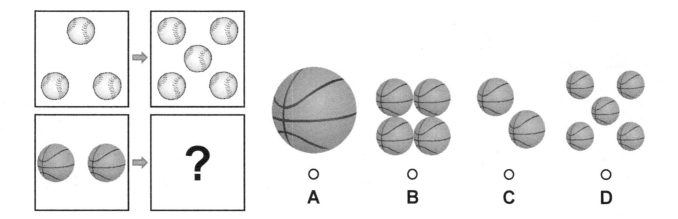

Question 11

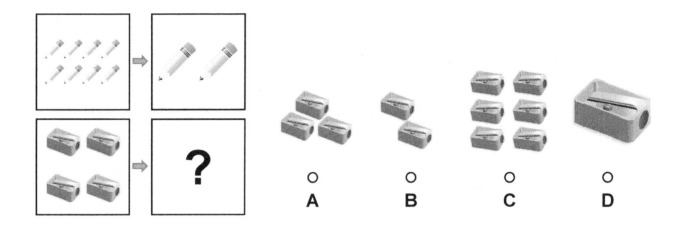

Question 12

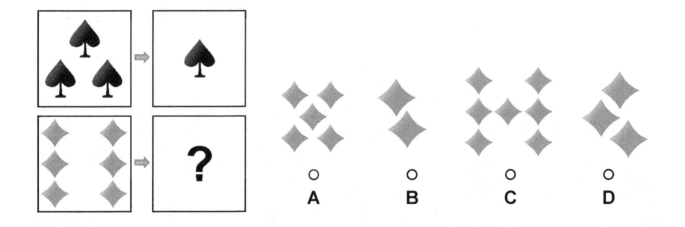

Question 13

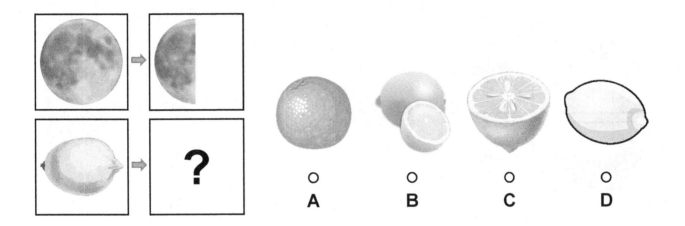

Question 14

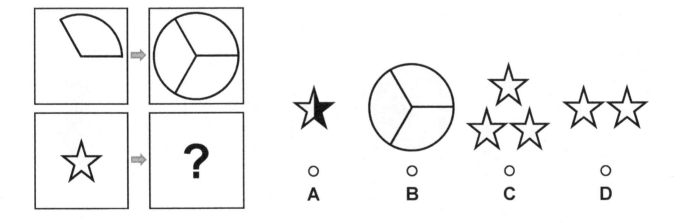

Question 15

○ A   ○ B   ○ C   ○ D

Question 16

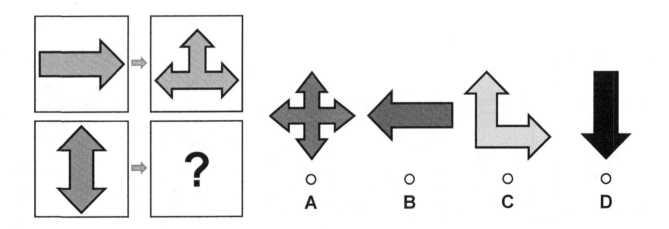

○ A   ○ B   ○ C   ○ D

Question 17

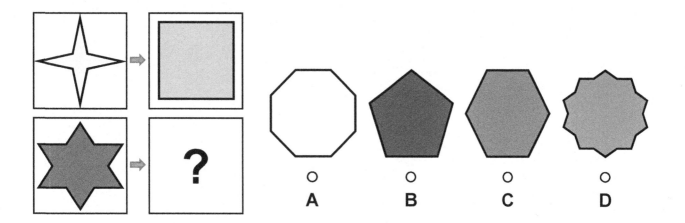

Question 18

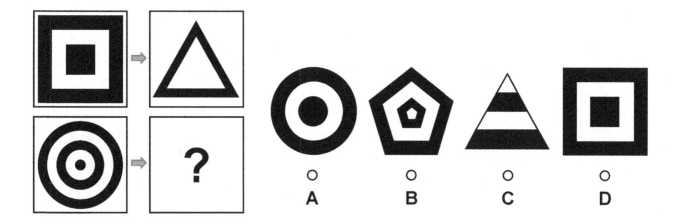

NUMBER PUZZLES

DIRECTIONS & EXAMPLE QUESTION

The following directions are to be used for all number puzzles questions:

Directions: The first train has a certain number of objects. Choose the answer choice that would give the second train the same total number of objects as the first train has.

Below is an example number puzzles question:

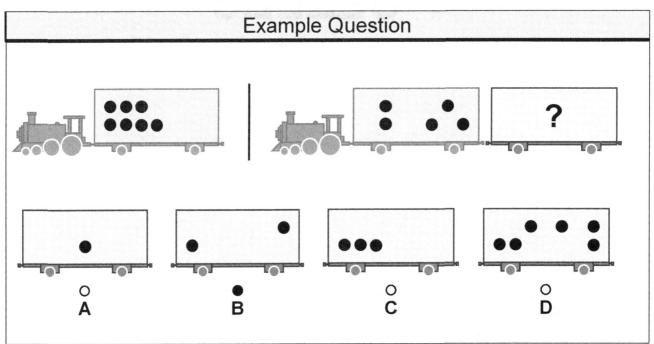

Example Question

Explanation: The first train contains 7 objects. The second train contains 5 objects. It needs 2 more objects (7 − 5 = 2 or 5 + 2 = 7) in order to have the same number of objects as the first train does.

Question 1

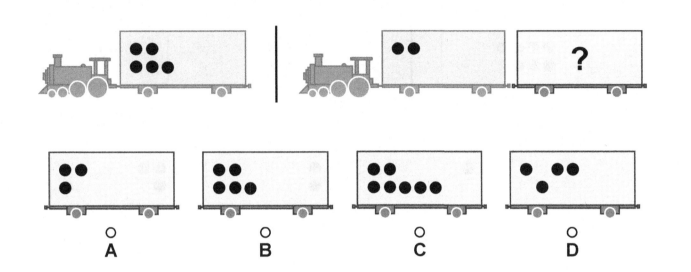

A   B   C   D

Question 2

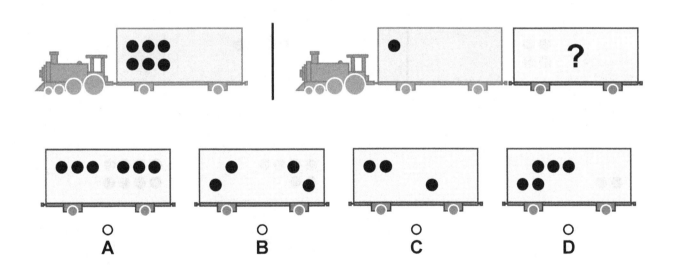

A   B   C   D

Question 3

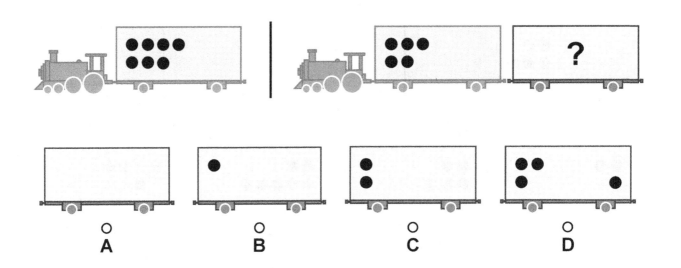

○
A

○
B

○
C

○
D

Question 4

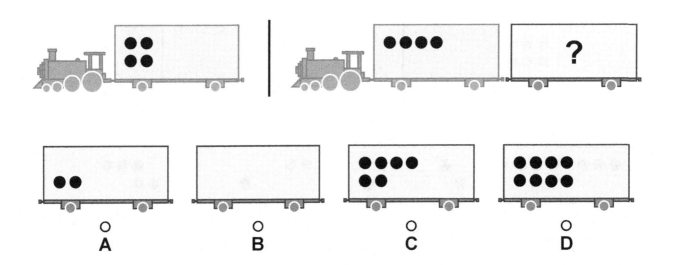

○
A

○
B

○
C

○
D

Question 5

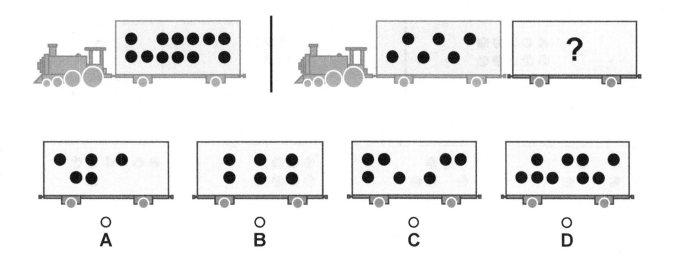

Question 6

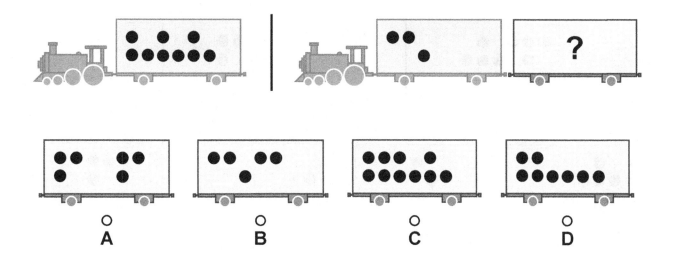

Question 7

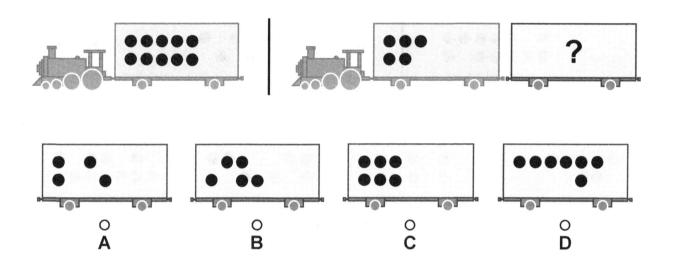

Question 8

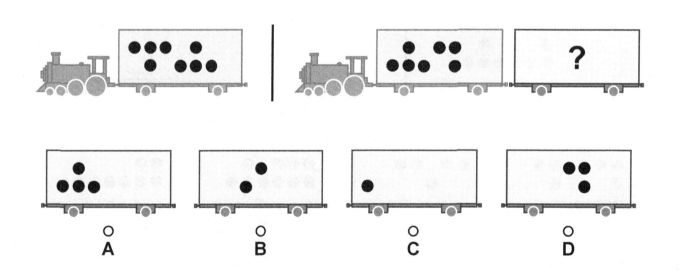

Question 9

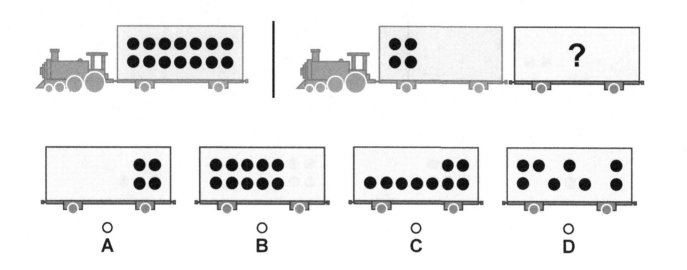

A   B   C   D

Question 10

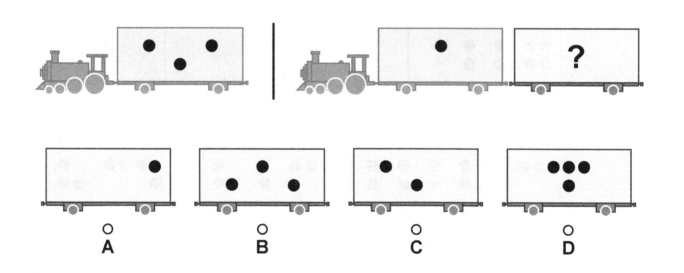

A   B   C   D

Question 11

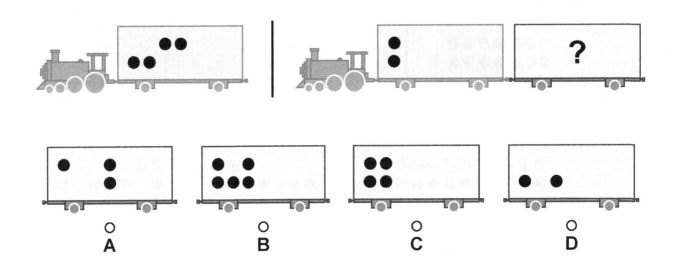

Question 12

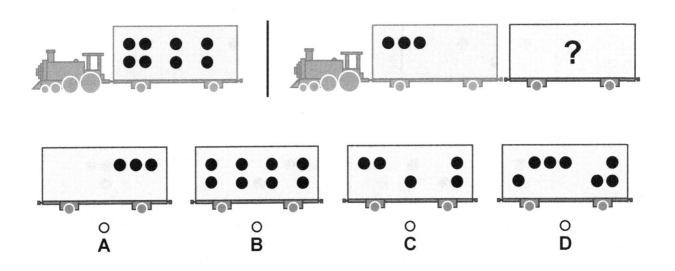

Question 13

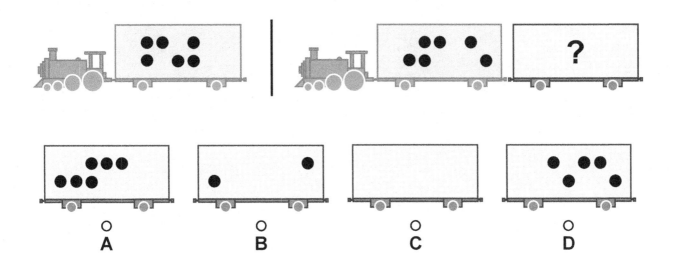

Question 14

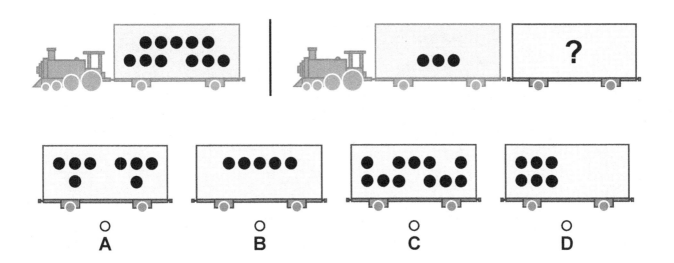

NUMBER
SERIES

Directions & Example Question

The following directions are to be used for all number series questions:

> **Directions:** In each question, an abacus is shown. The numbers of beads in the rows of the abacus form a pattern. Choose the answer choice that best continues the pattern in the next column of beads.

Below is an example number series question:

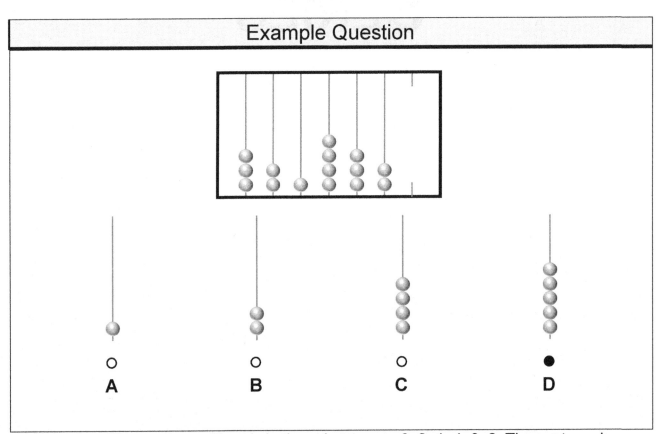

Explanation: The numbers of beads in the columns are: 3, 2, 1, 4, 3, 2. The next number should be 5, which is represented by D, because the next three numbers in the pattern are 5, 4, 3.

Question 1

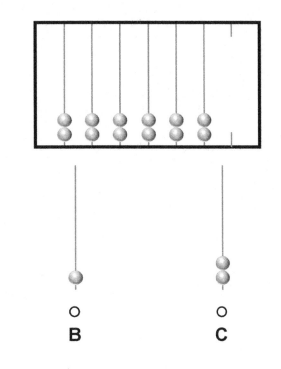

○
A

○
B

○
C

○
D

Question 2

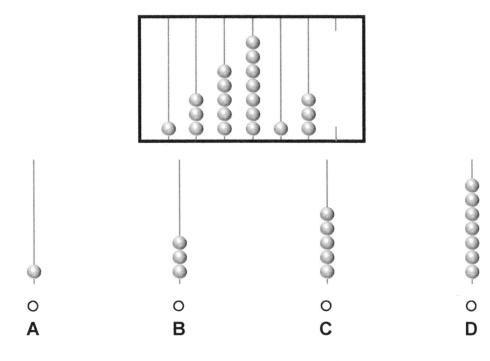

○
A

○
B

○
C

○
D

Question 3

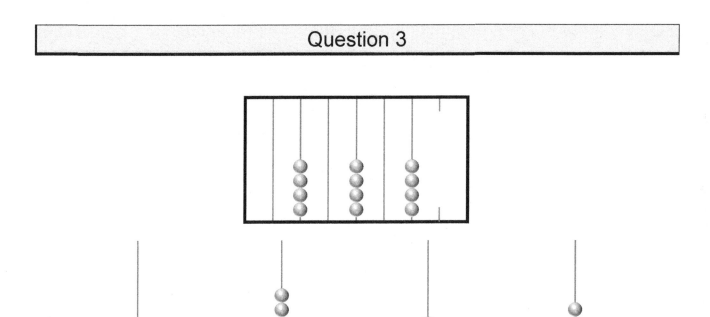

Question 4

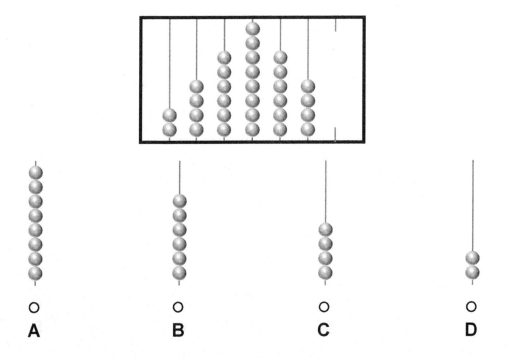

Question 5

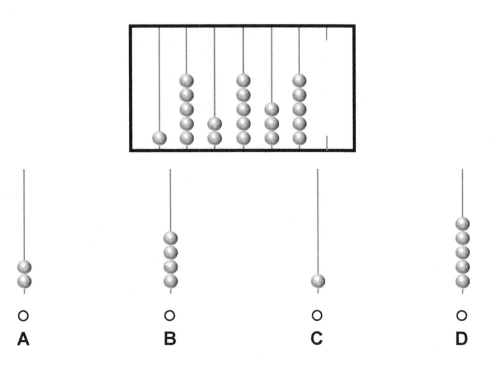

O
A

O
B

O
C

O
D

Question 6

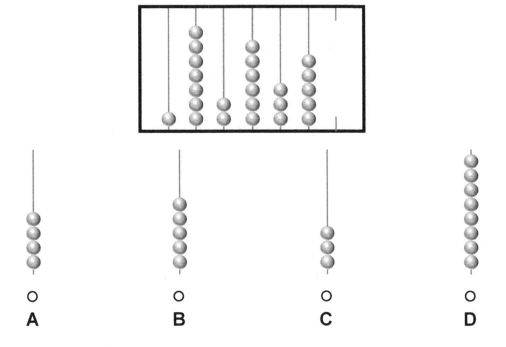

O
A

O
B

O
C

O
D

Question 7

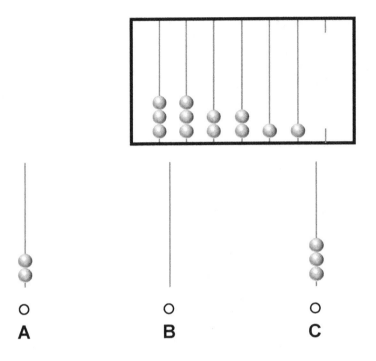

Question 8

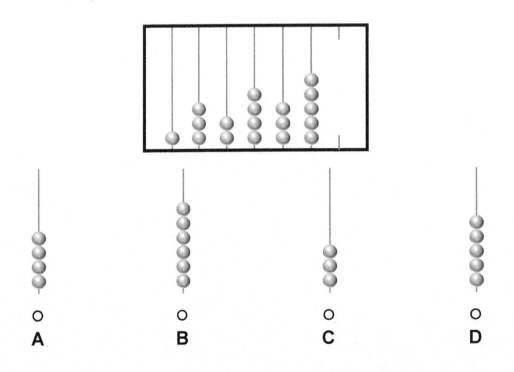

Question 9

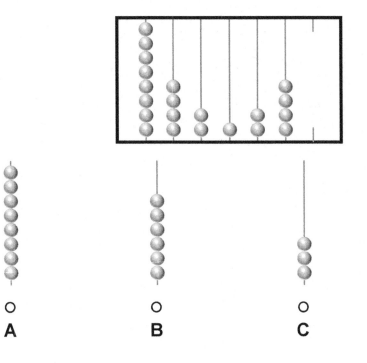

| A | B | C | D |

Question 10

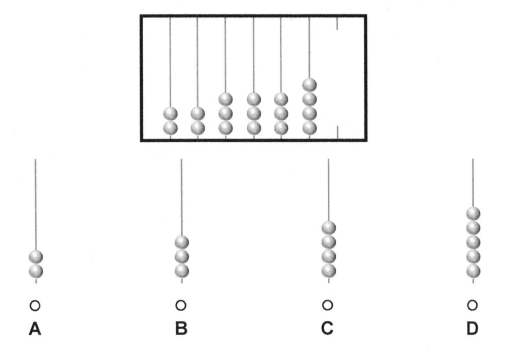

| A | B | C | D |

Question 11

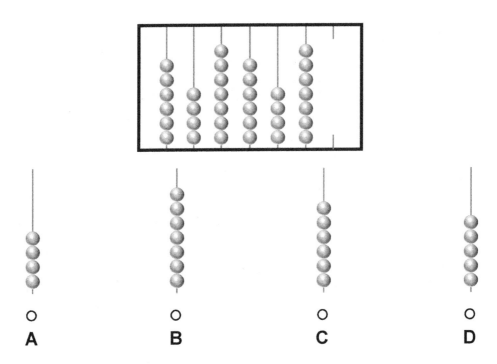

Question 12

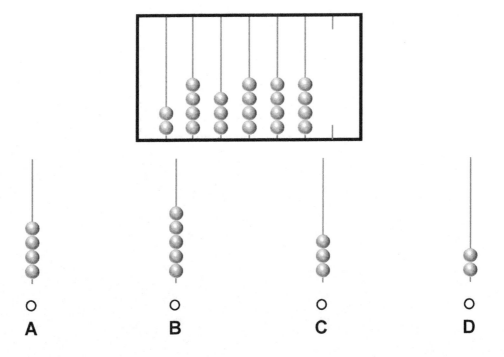

Question 13

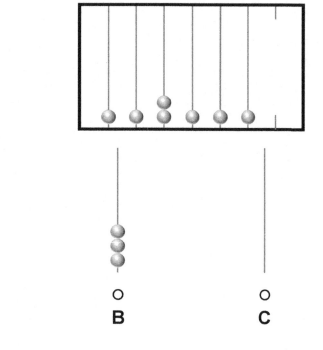

| A | B | C | D |

Question 14

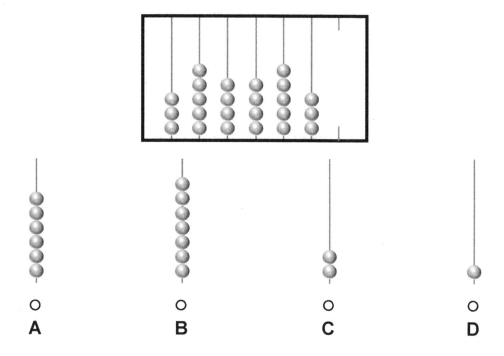

| A | B | C | D |

Question 15

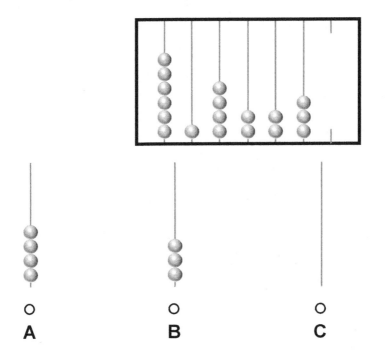

A   B   C   D

Question 16

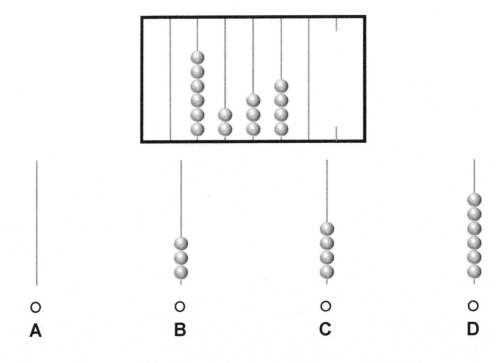

A   B   C   D

Question 17

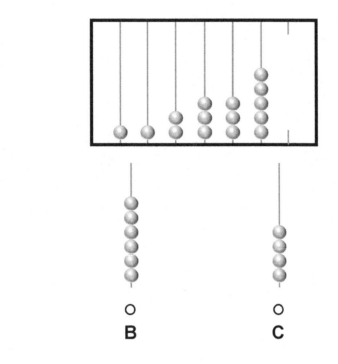

A   B   C   D

Question 18

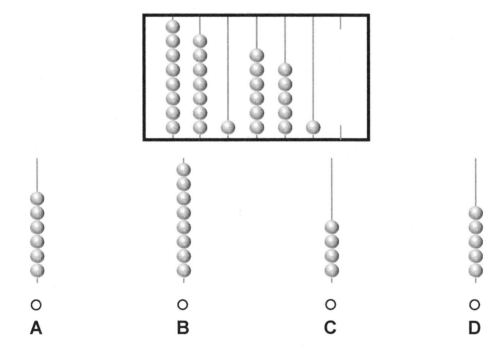

A   B   C   D

NONVERBAL
Battery

FIGURE
MATRICES

DIRECTIONS & EXAMPLE QUESTION

The following directions are to be used for all figure matrices questions:

Directions: For each question, in the grid of four squares, the top two figures go together. Choose the answer choice that goes with the bottom left figure.

Below is an example figure matrices question:

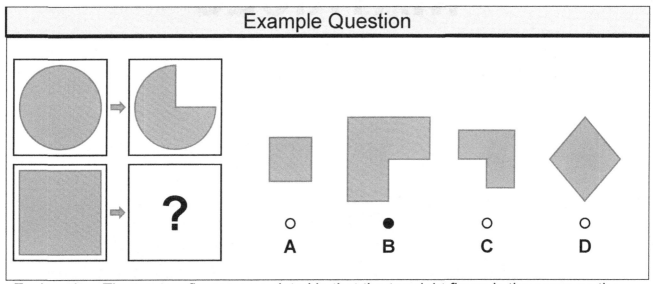

Explanation: The top two figures are related in that the top right figure is the same as the top left figure but with a quarter of the figure removed. The answer choice B is the same as the bottom left figure except with a quarter of the square removed. C is not correct because it is not the same size as the bottom left figure.

Question 1

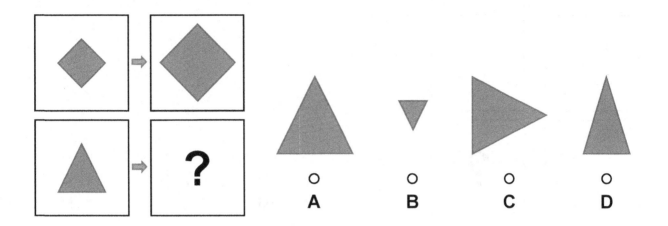

Question 2

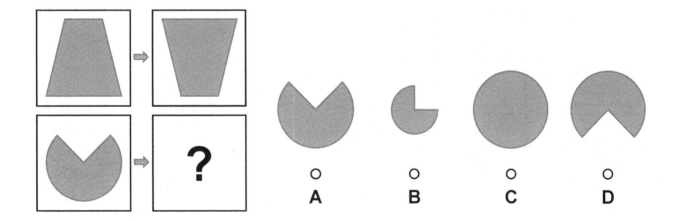

Question 3

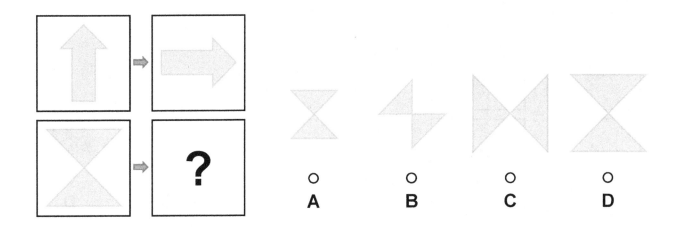

Question 4

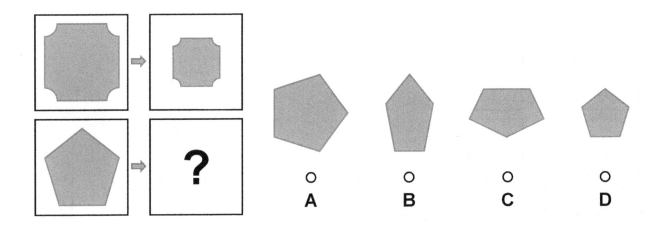

Question 5

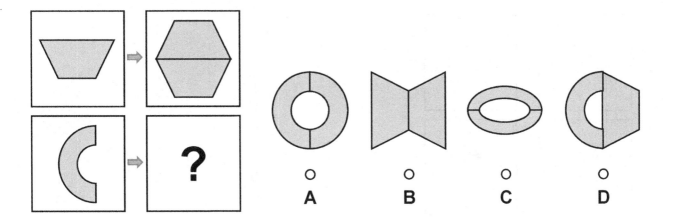

Question 6

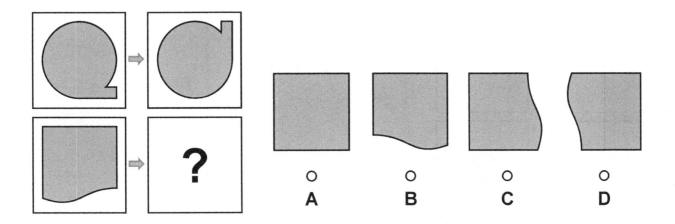

Question 7

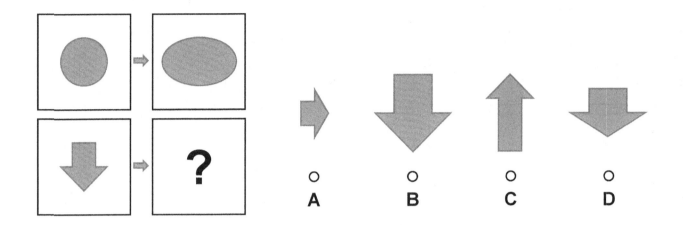

Question 8

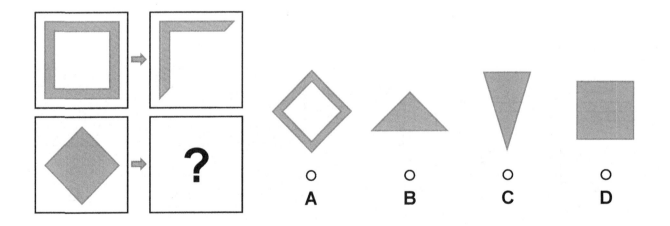

Question 9

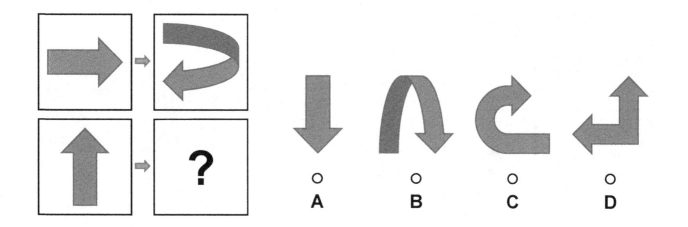

Question 10

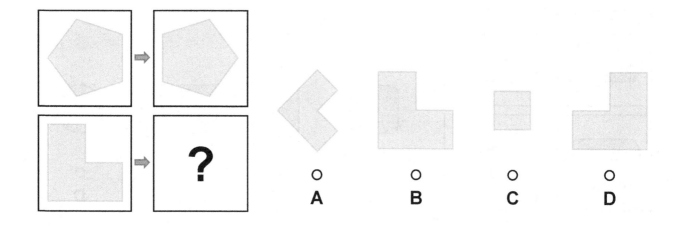

Question 11

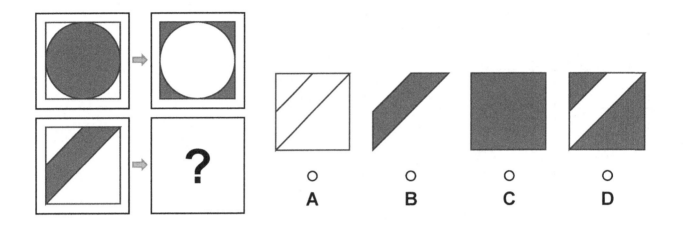

Question 12

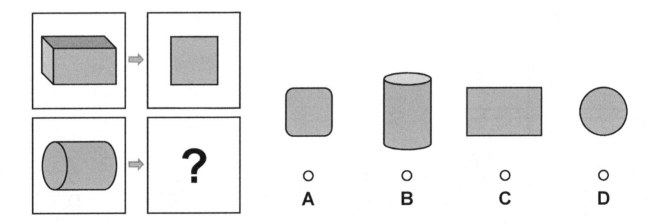

Question 13

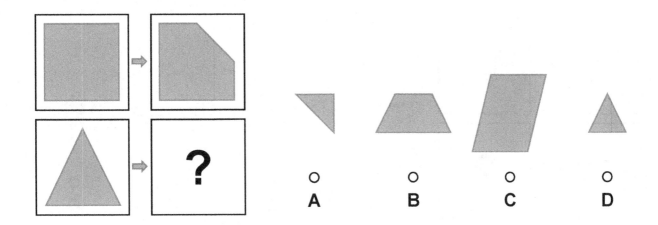

Question 14

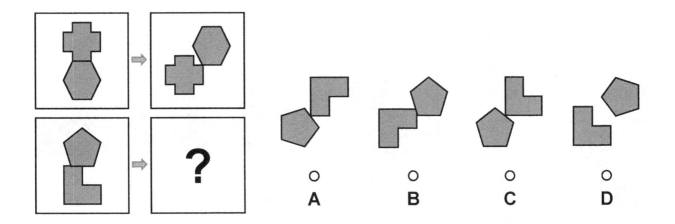

Question 15

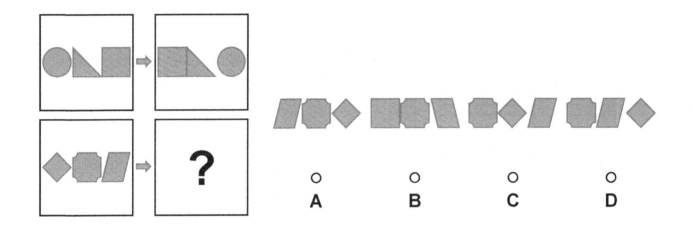

Question 16

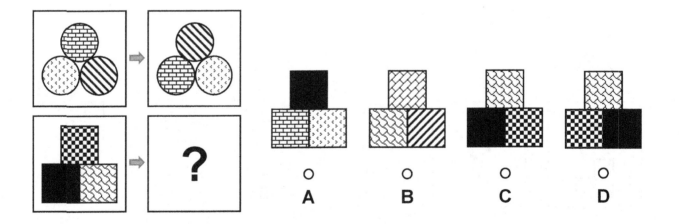

Question 17

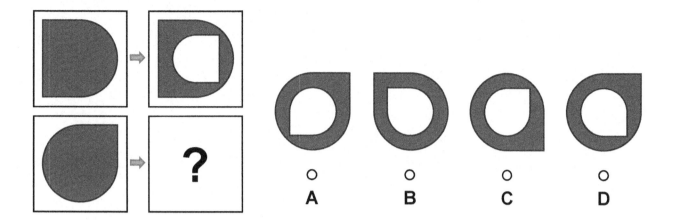

Question 18

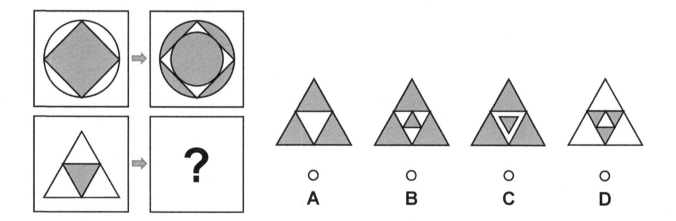

PAPER
FOLDING

DIRECTIONS & EXAMPLE QUESTION

The following directions are to be used for all paper folding questions:

Directions: In each question, a square piece of paper is folded. After it is folded all the way, holes are punched into the paper. You must figure out what the paper will look like when it is completely unfolded.

Below is an example paper folding question:

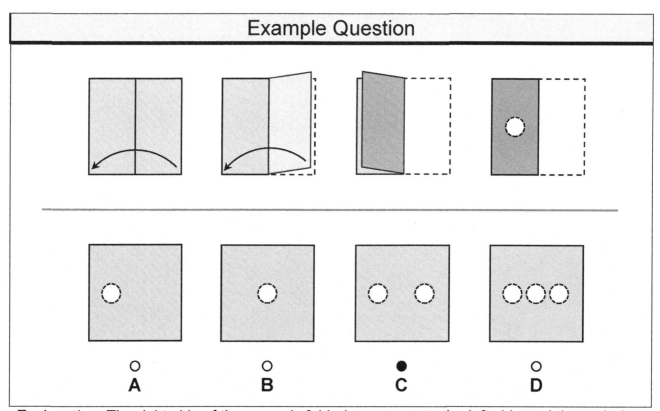

Explanation: The right side of the paper is folded over once to the left side and then a hole is punched in. Because there is only one fold, the paper will have two holes when it is completely unfolded. Thus, C must be the correct answer.

Question 1

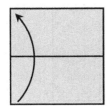 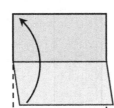 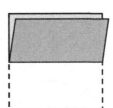 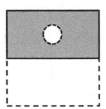

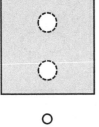  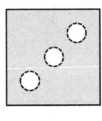 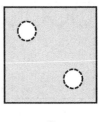

| A | B | C | D |

Question 2

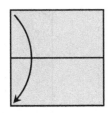 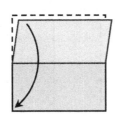 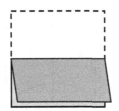 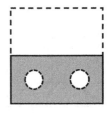

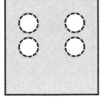   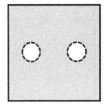

| A | B | C | D |

139

Question 3

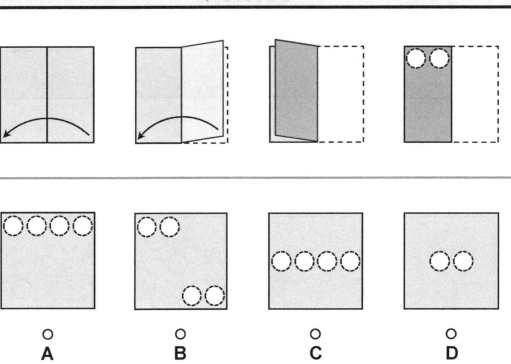

○
A

○
B

○
C

○
D

Question 4

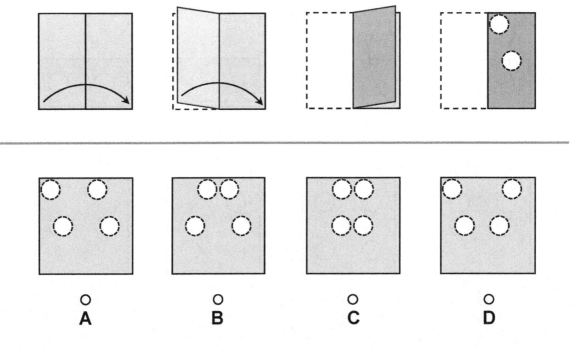

○
A

○
B

○
C

○
D

Question 5

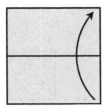 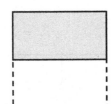 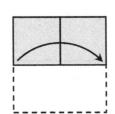 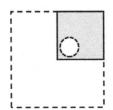

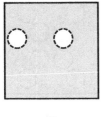 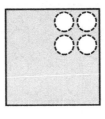 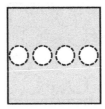 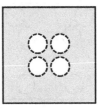

A

○
B

○
C

○
D

Question 6

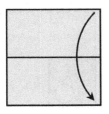 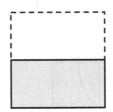 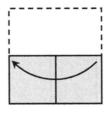 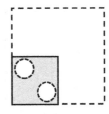

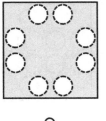 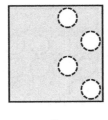 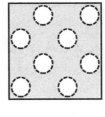 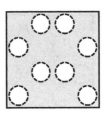

A

○
B

○
C

○
D

Question 7

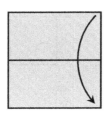  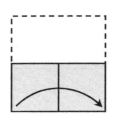 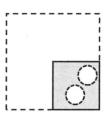

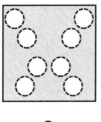 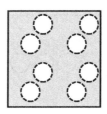 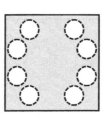 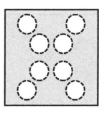

A
○
B
○
C
○
D

Question 8

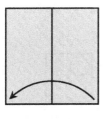 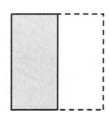 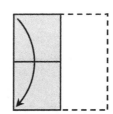 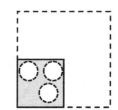

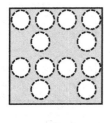 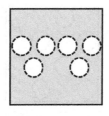 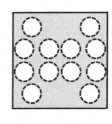 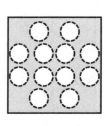

○
A
○
B
○
C
○
D

Question 9

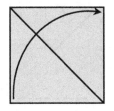 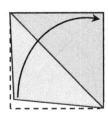 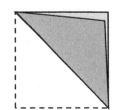 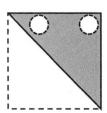

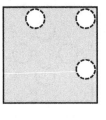 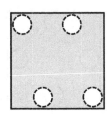 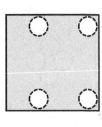 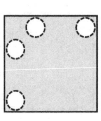

A
B
C
D

Question 10

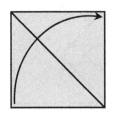 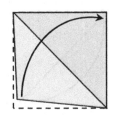 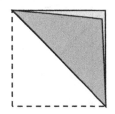 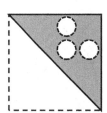

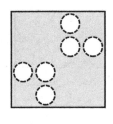 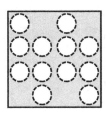 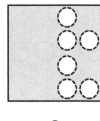 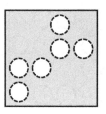

A
B
C
D

Question 11

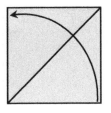 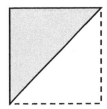 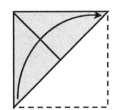 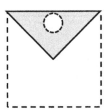

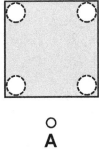 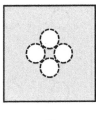 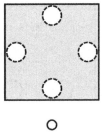 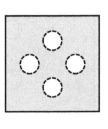

○   ○   ○   ○
A   **B**   **C**   **D**

Question 12

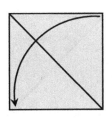 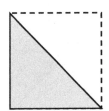 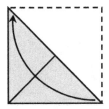 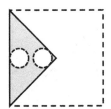

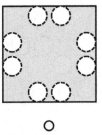 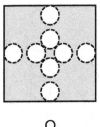 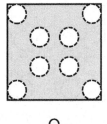 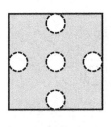

○   ○   ○   ○
A   **B**   **C**   **D**

Question 13

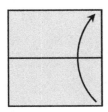 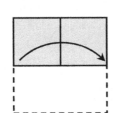 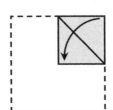 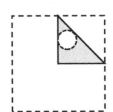

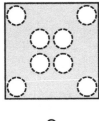 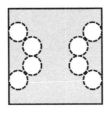 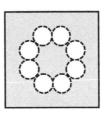 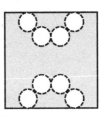

○
A

○
B

○
C

○
D

Question 14

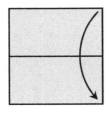 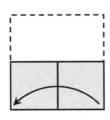 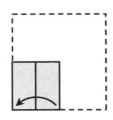 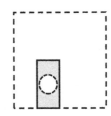

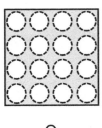 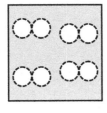 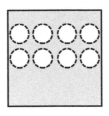 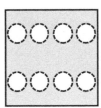

○
A

○
B

○
C

○
D

FIGURE CLASSIFICATION

DIRECTIONS & EXAMPLE QUESTION

The following directions are to be used for all figure classification questions:

Directions: In each question, the first three figures in the top row are alike in one or more ways. Choose the figure from the bottom row that most belongs with the figures in the top row.

Below is an example figure classification question:

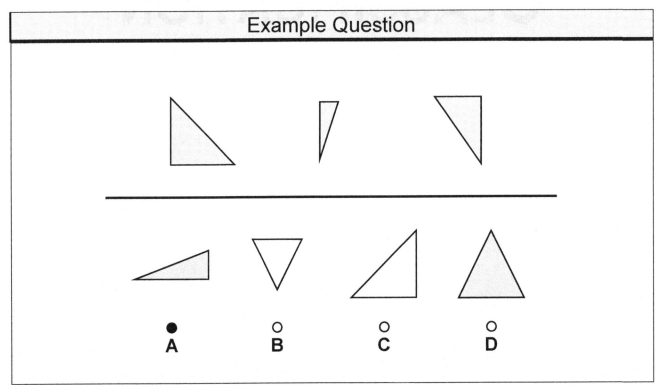

Explanation: All three of the figures in the top row are shaded and have a right angle, meaning two sides meet perpendicularly, as if to form a corner of a rectangle. Thus, A is correct. C is not correct because it is not shaded. D is not correct because it does not have a right angle.

Question 1

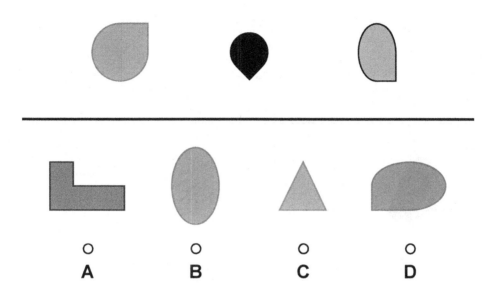

Question 2

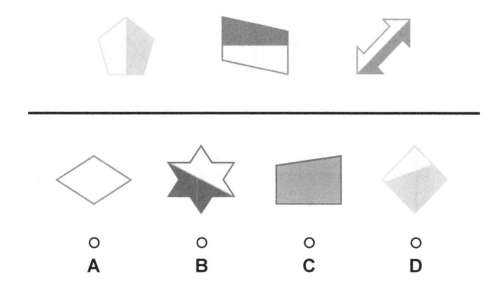

Question 3

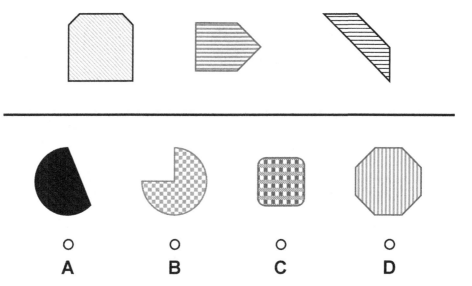

Question 4

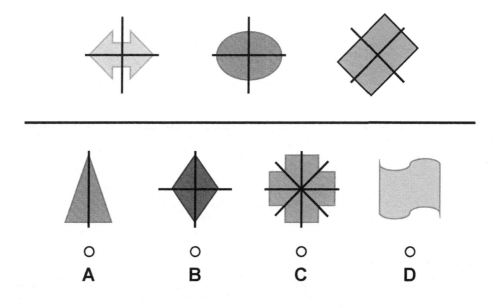

Question 5

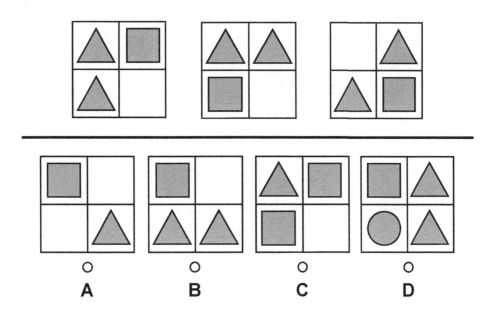

Question 6

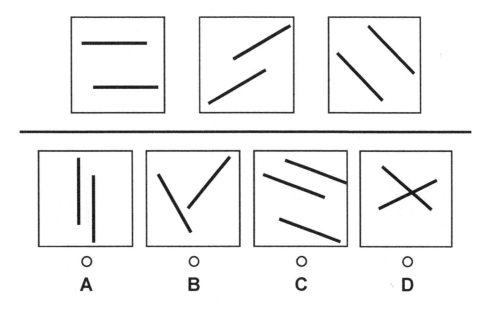

Question 7

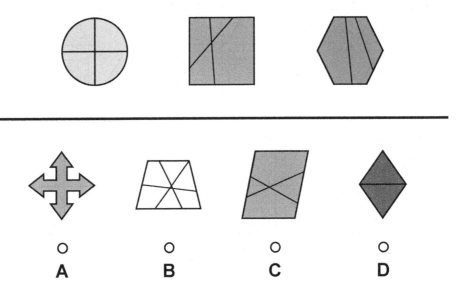

A	B	C	D
○	○	○	○

Question 8

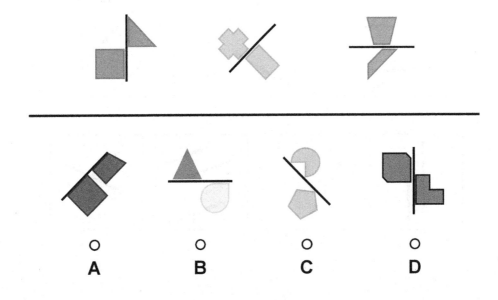

A	B	C	D
○	○	○	○

Question 9

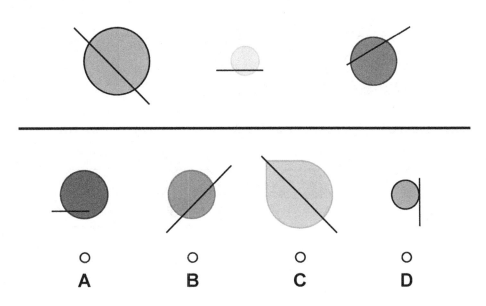

○ **A** ○ **B** ○ **C** ○ **D**

Question 10

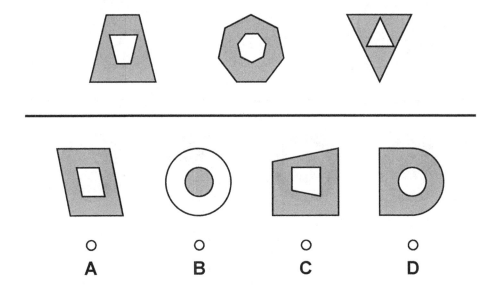

○ **A** ○ **B** ○ **C** ○ **D**

Question 11

○   ○   ○   ○

A   **B**   **C**   **D**

Question 12

○   ○   ○   ○

A   **B**   **C**   **D**

Question 13

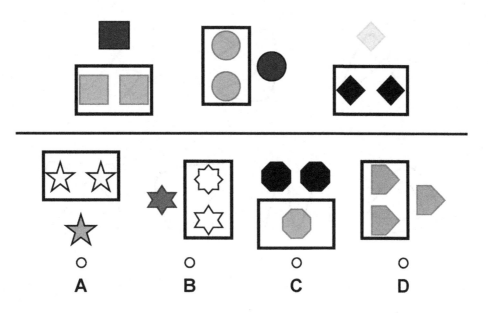

Question 14

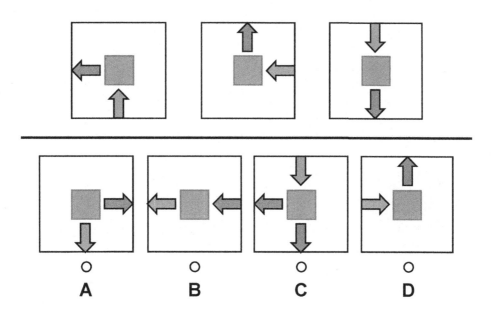

Question 15

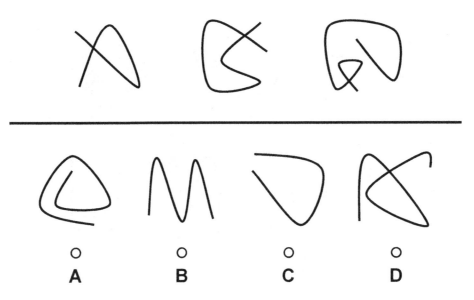

Question 16

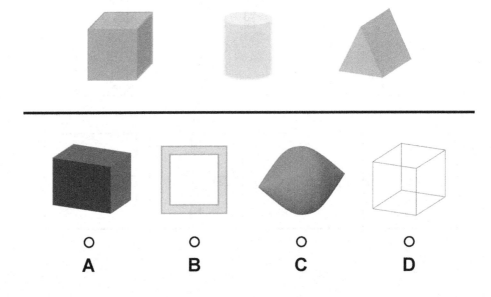

Question 17

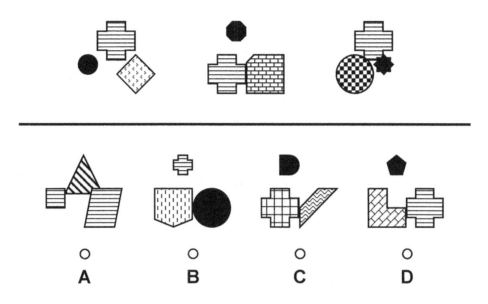

○
A

○
B

○
C

○
D

Question 18

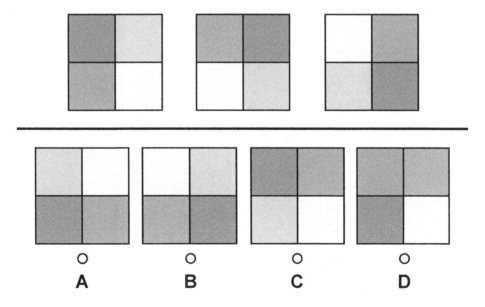

○
A

○
B

○
C

○
D

ANSWERS
& Explanations

ANSWER KEYS

VERBAL BATTERY
Answer Key

Directions: For each question, record your answer in the column where it says "Your Answer", next to the number of the question. If your answer does not match the correct answer, mark an 'X' in the column labeled "X". Afterwards, tally the total number of incorrect answers. Subtract this amount from the total number of questions to find the total number of correct answers per subtest. Multiply the number correct by 5.56%, if there are 18 questions, or by 7.14%, if there are 14 questions, in order to get the percent correct for each subtest.

Verbal Analogies

#	Correct Answer	Your Answer	X
1	A		
2	D		
3	A		
4	D		
5	B		
6	C		
7	B		
8	C		
9	B		
10	C		
11	D		
12	D		
13	A		
14	A		
15	B		
16	A		
17	A		
18	C		

Sentence Completion

#	Correct Answer	Your Answer	X
1	D		
2	C		
3	B		
4	A		
5	B		
6	B		
7	B		
8	A		
9	B		
10	D		
11	A		
12	A		
13	D		
14	B		
15	D		
16	C		
17	B		
18	A		

Verbal Classification

#	Correct Answer	Your Answer	X
1	B		
2	D		
3	C		
4	C		
5	D		
6	C		
7	B		
8	B		
9	D		
10	D		
11	B		
12	C		
13	B		
14	A		
15	C		
16	A		
17	C		
18	B		

Total Incorrect: _____   **Total Incorrect:** _____   **Total Incorrect:** _____

Total Correct: _____   **Total Correct:** _____   **Total Correct:** _____

Percent Correct: _____   **Percent Correct:** _____   **Percent Correct:** _____

QUANTITATIVE BATTERY
Answer Key

Directions: For each question, record your answer in the column where it says "Your Answer", next to the number of the question. If your answer does not match the correct answer, mark an 'X' in the column labeled "X". Afterwards, tally the total number of incorrect answers. Subtract this amount from the total number of questions to find the total number of correct answers per subtest. Multiply the number correct by 5.56%, if there are 18 questions, or by 7.14%, if there are 14 questions, in order to get the percent correct for each subtest.

Number Analogies

#	Correct Answer	Your Answer	X
1	A		
2	D		
3	C		
4	A		
5	D		
6	D		
7	D		
8	A		
9	C		
10	B		
11	D		
12	B		
13	C		
14	C		
15	C		
16	A		
17	C		
18	B		

Number Puzzles

#	Correct Answer	Your Answer	X
1	A		
2	D		
3	C		
4	B		
5	B		
6	A		
7	B		
8	C		
9	B		
10	C		
11	D		
12	C		
13	C		
14	A		

Number Series

#	Correct Answer	Your Answer	X
1	C		
2	C		
3	A		
4	D		
5	B		
6	A		
7	B		
8	A		
9	A		
10	C		
11	C		
12	B		
13	B		
14	A		
15	C		
16	D		
17	C		
18	C		

Total Incorrect: _____   Total Incorrect: _____   Total Incorrect: _____

Total Correct: _____   Total Correct: _____   Total Correct: _____

Percent Correct: _____   Percent Correct: _____   Percent Correct: _____

NONVERBAL BATTERY
Answer Key

Directions: For each question, record your answer in the column where it says "Your Answer", next to the number of the question. If your answer does not match the correct answer, mark an 'X' in the column labeled "X". Afterwards, tally the total number of incorrect answers. Subtract this amount from the total number of questions to find the total number of correct answers per subtest. Multiply the number correct by 5.56%, if there are 18 questions, or by 7.14%, if there are 14 questions, in order to get the percent correct for each subtest.

Figure Matrices

#	Correct Answer	Your Answer	X
1	A		
2	D		
3	C		
4	D		
5	A		
6	C		
7	D		
8	B		
9	B		
10	D		
11	D		
12	D		
13	B		
14	C		
15	A		
16	D		
17	A		
18	B		

Total Incorrect: _____

Total Correct: _____

Percent Correct: _____

Paper Folding

#	Correct Answer	Your Answer	X
1	A		
2	B		
3	A		
4	B		
5	D		
6	A		
7	C		
8	D		
9	D		
10	A		
11	C		
12	B		
13	D		
14	D		

Total Incorrect: _____

Total Correct: _____

Percent Correct: _____

Figure Classification

#	Correct Answer	Your Answer	X
1	D		
2	B		
3	D		
4	B		
5	B		
6	A		
7	C		
8	D		
9	B		
10	C		
11	B		
12	A		
13	A		
14	D		
15	D		
16	A		
17	D		
18	A		

Total Incorrect: _____

Total Correct: _____

Percent Correct: _____

ANSWER EXPLANATIONS

VERBAL BATTERY
Explanations

Verbal Analogies

1. **A**. A snail is slow, and a rabbit is fast. The best choice is A because it depicts someone in the act of running, which is fast. The analogy would therefore be snail is to rabbit as crawling is to running.

2. **D**. A skyscraper is much taller than a house. A giraffe is much taller than a mouse. Choice A and Choice C are not correct because a skyscraper and a house are both buildings, so the best answer choice should be an animal.

3. **A**. A bird eats worms, and a fox eats rabbits.

4. **D**. A grasshopper is an insect, and so is a ladybug. A lizard is a reptile, and so is crocodile. Choice C is not correct because a frog is an amphibian, not a reptile.

5. **B**. An airplane flies, and so does a butterfly. A scuba diver swims, and so does a whale. Choice D is incorrect because clams do not swim. They are mostly immobile because they have no method of propulsion. Also, instead of clam, if we answered this question using shells, then the logic still holds. Shells do not swim, so B is the best choice.

6. **C**. Corn grows on corn stalks. Apples grow on apple trees.

7. **B**. A sun is a symbol of summer, and trees have green leaves in the summer. Snow is a symbol of winter, and many trees do not have leaves in the winter. Winter is the only time trees normally and naturally do not have their leaves. Choices C and D are incorrect because they're not as close in relationship to the first pair, which involved a tree, even though a scarf and holly may represent winter.

8. **C**. A bookshelf holds books. A toolbox holds tools, such as a wrench.

9. **B**. A spider has 8 legs, and an octagon has 8 sides. An ant has 6 legs, and a hexagon has 6 sides.

10. **C**. A frog lives in a pond, and a bird lives in a nest.

11. **D**. A golf club is used to hit a golf ball. A tennis racket is used to hit a tennis ball.

12. **D**. A drum set is played with drumsticks. A violin is played with a violin bow.

13. **A**. A surfboard is used to play at the beach. A sled is used to play in snow covered hills. The other choices show outer space, a tropical island, and a forest.

14. **A**. A chicken leg comes from a chicken. Bacon comes from a pig. Choice D is incorrect because eggs do not come from pigs. That is, pigs do not lay eggs.

15. **B**. A pencil and an eraser are frequently used together when writing. More specifically, the pencil is the tool that touches the paper or writing surface to produce the writing. An eraser is not a direct production tool or implement, as it doesn't produce the writing directly. A paintbrush and a palette are both used together for painting. The paintbrush is the primary tool that touches the canvas or painting surface to produce the painting. Like the eraser, the palette is not a direct production tool. That is, it does not directly cause the painting to materialize. Choice C is incorrect because it is not as good of an answer choice as B is. Even if a painter uses pencils or colored pencils together with the paintbrush (painters often sketch before they paint), the palette is not another direct production tool, whereas colored pencils are.

16. **A**. A construction worker wears a hard hat to protect his head. He uses a hammer to do his work. A knight wears a helmet to protect his hat, and he uses a sword to do his work, which is to fight.

17. **A**. A duck hatches from an egg. A tree grows from an acorn. Choice B is incorrect because it is not as directly analogous. Leaves don't sprout from acorns directly.

18. **C**. An astronaut works on a space shuttle. A captain works on a ship.

Sentence Completion

1. **D**. Birds have wings. Salamanders, deer, and sea turtles do not have wings.

2. **C**. Colored pencils are used for drawing. Staplers, spatulas, and paperclips are not used for drawing.

3. **B**. Desks are commonly found in classrooms. Cars, bowling balls, and garden hoses are not typically found in classrooms.

4. **A**. Larger objects are usually heavier than smaller objects. An elephant is much larger than a dumbbell, a brick, and a feather, and it is also much heavier.

5. **B**. Computer keyboards are not used for cooking. Pans, blenders, and spoons are used for cooking.

6. **B**. Snakes live in the desert. Bears, fish, and flamingoes do not typically live in the desert.

7. **B**. Mountains are much taller than giraffes, palm trees, and dog houses.

8. **A**. Treadmills are used for exercise. Couches, hamburgers, and computers are typically not used to exercise.

9. **B**. Crabs have claws. Sharks, horses, and flies do not have claws.

10. **D**. A sieve drains water from food because it has holes in it. A tennis racket has holes, but it is not used with food, so choice B is incorrect. Neither spoons nor pots are used for draining water from foods. Even if it might be difficult for a student to identify a sieve, process of elimination makes D the best choice.

11. **A**. A dessert is usually a sweet food for the last course of a meal. Cupcakes or cakes are birthday dessert items, usually. Pizzas and hot dogs are not typically eaten for dessert and are considered entrées. While a candy cane is a sweet and can be a dessert, it's more likely kids will have cupcakes at a birthday party.

12. **A**. Venomous means that the animal can poison another animal with a bite or a sting. Cobras are venomous animals. Koalas, seals, and lions are not venomous.

13. **D**. Buses are used for transportation. Laundry machines, chairs, and cats are not used for transportation.

14. **B**. Nocturnal means that the animal is active at night and sleeps during the day. Bats are nocturnal. Squirrels, cows, and pigeons are not nocturnal.

15. **D**. Tape measures are used for measuring length. Choice B is not as good as choice D because calculators do not directly measure length, although they can be used for helping someone to figure out the combined length of multiple objects.

16. **C**. A glue gun is used for repairing. Bombs, broken eggshells, and shoes are not used for repairing. Even if the student has never seen a glue gun before, this is the most logical answer to choose by elimination. Learning this skill set will help the student avoid potential mistakes later on, if he or she encounters unfamiliar images or words.

17. **B**. An object that is found in the sky is not touching the ground or water. A cloud is in the sky and is not touching the ground. The Eiffel tower, a boat, and a tree are not found in the sky because they are touching the ground or water.

18. **A**. An alarm clock is used to wake people up.

Verbal Classification

1. **B**. The top row shows a soccer goal, a basketball hoop, and a baseball home plate. These are all goals in sports. A football field goal is also a goal.

2. **D**. The top row shows a fork, a knife, and a straw. These are all eating utensils. A spoon is also an eating utensil.

3. **C**. The top row shows a stingray, a beaver, and a turtle. These all spend significant parts of their lives, or all of their lives, underwater. A frog also spends a significant portion of its life in water.

4. **C**. The top row shows a beach ball, a top, and a yo-yo. These are all toys. A slinky is also a toy.

5. **D**. The top row shows a water gun, beach towel, and snorkeling goggles, things one might bring to the beach for recreational purposes. A pail and shovel is an item that might be brought to the beach to build sand castles with. A shell would be picked up and found at the beach, but it is probably not going to be brought to the beach. Similarly, lobsters and palm trees may be naturally found at some beaches, but they wouldn't be brought to the beach.

6. **C**. The top row shows a planet, a star, and a comet. These are all natural objects found in space. An asteroid is also a natural object found in space. Choice B is not correct because a spaceship is not a natural object.

7. **B**. The top row shows coffee, water, and a strawberry smoothie. These are all drinks. Lemonade is also a drink.

8. **B**. The top row shows a box cutter, a nail, and a broken bottle. These are all sharp. Scissors are also sharp.

9. **D**. The top row shows a drinking glass, glasses, and binoculars. These all contain glass. A window is also made of glass. Choice B is wrong. Even though it is a cup, it looks like the plastic cups commonly found in supermarkets.

10. **D**. The top row shows a jacket, earmuffs, and a winter hat. These are all winter clothing. Choices A and D both show winter clothing—boots and gloves, respectively. D, however, is the better choice because it is worn on the upper body, just as jackets, earmuffs, and hats are.

11. **B**. The top row shows a stem, roots, and a flower. These are all parts of a flower. A leaf is also a part of a flower. Choice A is not correct because it shows a bouquet, which is a collection of flowers, but not a part of a flower.

12. **C**. The top row shows a pig, a sheep, and a chicken. These are all farm animals. A cow is also a farm animal.

13. **B**. The top row shows rice, bread, and macaroni. These are all grains. Cereal is also a grain.

14. **A**. The top row shows a fire, a toaster, and the sun. These are all hot. An iron is also hot.

15. **C**. The top row shows a crate, a cabinet, and a binder. These are all used to store physical objects. A safe is also used to store physical objects. Choice A is incorrect because a computer is not used to store physical objects, although it can be used to store digital objects, such as electronic files.

16. **A**. The top row shows a tornado, a volcano, and a flood. These are all natural disasters. Choice A shows an earthquake, which is also a natural disaster. Choice C is incorrect because it is not a natural disaster. Choice B is incorrect because a campfire is not considered a natural disaster.

17. **C**. The top row shows a hat, headphones, and sunglasses. These are all worn on the head. A hard hat is also worn on the head.

18. **B**. The top row shows gold, jewelry, and a sports car. These are all expensive objects. A diamond is also an expensive object.

QUANTITATIVE BATTERY
Explanations

Number Analogies

1. **A.** 4 leaves decreases to 3 (4 − 1 = 3) leaves, so 2 leaves should be decreased to 1 (2 − 1 = 1) leaf.

2. **D.** 2 squares are increased to 5 (2 + 3 = 5) squares, so 1 circle should be increased to 4 (1 + 3 = 4) circles.

3. **C.** 5 mice are decreased to 3 (5 − 2 = 3) mice, so 3 cheese wedges should be decreased to 1 (3 − 2 = 1) cheese wedges.

4. **A.** The number of dots on the die equals the number of cookies. The correct answer is 2 cupcakes because the number of dots on the die in the third figure is 2.

5. **D.** 2 books are doubled to 4 books, so 3 books should be doubled to 6 books.

6. **D.** The first figure shows 2 cars. Half of 2 cars is 1 car. Add 1 car to 2 cars and get 3 cars. Half of 4 cars is 2 cars. Add 2 cars to 4 cars and get 6 cars.

7. **D.** 1 strawberry is increased to 4 (1 + 3 = 4) strawberries, so 2 bananas should be increased to 5 (2 + 3 = 5).

8. **A.** 2 moons are halved to 1 moon, so 4 clouds should be halved to 2 clouds.

9. **C.** 1 quarter circle is quadrupled to 4 quarter circles, so 1 puzzle piece should be quadrupled to 4 puzzle pieces.

10. **B.** 3 baseballs are increased to 5 (3 + 2 = 5) baseballs, so 2 basketballs should be increased to 4 (2 + 2 = 4) basketballs.

11. **D.** 8 pencils are halved once to get 4 pencils, then halved again to get 2 pencils. 4 pencil sharpeners should be halved once to get 2 pencil sharpeners, then halved again to get 1 pencil sharpener.

12. **B.** If 3 spades are separated into 3 groups of 1 spade each, then 1 of those groups would be 1 spade. If 6 diamonds are separated into 3 groups of 2 diamonds each, then 1 of those groups would be 2 diamonds.

13. **C.** 1 moon is halved to half of a moon, so 1 lemon should be halved to half of a lemon.

14. **C.** 1 third of a circle is increased to 3 (1 + 2 = 3) thirds of a circle, so 1 star should be increased to 3 (1 + 2 = 3) stars.

15. **C.** The first figure shows a spider, which has 8 legs. The second figure shows an ant, which has 6 legs. The number of legs is decreased by 2 (8 − 2 = 6) legs. The third figure shows a lion, which has 4 legs, so the correct answer should show an animal that has 2 (4 − 2 = 2) legs, such as a flamingo.

16. **A.** 1 arrow is increased to 3 (1 + 2 = 3) arrows, so 2 arrows should be increased to 4 (2 + 2 = 4) arrows.

17. **C.** The first figure shows a star with 4 points, and the second figure shows a shape with 4 sides. The number of points and sides are equal. The third figure shows a star with 6 points, so the correct answer should show a shape with 6 sides, such as a hexagon.

18. **B.** The first figure shows a shape with 3 black and white bands, and the second figure shows a shape with 2 black and white bands. The number of bands is decreased by 1 (3 − 1 = 2) bands. The third figure shows a shape with 5 black and white bands, so the correct answer should show a shape with 4 (5 − 1 = 4) bands. Choice C is not the best answer because the bands in the question are all centered around the same point, but the bands in Choice C are not centered around a point.

Number Puzzles

1. **A.** The first train has 5 dots. The second train has 2, so it needs 3 more to make 5 (2 + 3 = 5).

2. **D.** The first train has 6 dots. The second train has 1, so it needs 5 more to make 6 (1 + 5 = 6).

3. **C.** The first train has 7 dots. The second train has 5, so it needs 2 more to make 7 (5 + 2 = 5).

4. **B.** The first train has 4 dots. The second train has 4, so it needs 0 more to make 4 (4 + 0 = 4).

5. **B.** The first train has 12 dots. The second train has 6, so it needs 6 more to make 12 (6 + 6 = 12).

6. **A.** The first train has 9 dots. The second train has 3, so it needs 6 more to make 9 (3 + 6 = 9).

7. **B.** The first train has 10 dots. The second train has 5, so it needs 5 more to make 10 (5 + 5 = 10).

8. **C.** The first train has 8 dots. The second train has 7, so it needs 1 more to make 8 (7 + 1 = 8).

9. **B.** The first train has 14 dots. The second train has 4, so it needs 10 more to make 14 (4 + 10 = 14).

10. **C.** The first train has 3 dots. The second train has 1, so it needs 2 more to make 3 (1 + 2 = 3).

11. **D.** The first train has 4 dots. The second train has 2, so it needs 2 more to make 4 (2 + 2 = 4).

12. **C.** The first train has 8 dots. The second train has 3, so it needs 5 more to make 8 (3 + 5 = 8).

13. **C.** The first train has 6 dots. The second train has 6, so it needs 0 more to make 6 (6 + 0 = 6).

14. **A.** The first train has 11 dots. The second train has 3, so it needs 8 more to make 11 (3 + 8 = 11).

Number Series

1. **C**. The pattern is 2, 2, 2, 2, 2, 2. Every column has 2 beads, so the next column should also have 2 beads.

2. **C**. The pattern is 1, 3, 5, 7, 1, 3. The pattern increases by 2, then repeats after 4 numbers, so the next number after 3 should be 5.

3. **A**. The pattern is 0, 4, 0, 4, 0, 4. The pattern alternates between 0 and 4, so the next number after 4 should be 0.

4. **D**. The pattern is 2, 4, 6, 8, 6, 4. At first, the pattern increases by 2. After getting to 8, the pattern decreases by 2, so the next number after 4 should be 2.

5. **B**. The pattern is 1, 5, 2, 5, 3, 5. There are two patterns here. The odd columns (1, 2, 3) increase by 1. The even columns (5, 5, 5) are all 5, so the next number after 5 should be 4 (odd column; 3 + 1 = 4)

6. **A**. The pattern is 1, 7, 2, 6, 3, 5. There are two patterns here. The odd columns (1, 2, 3) increase by 1. The even columns (7, 6, 5) decrease by 1, so the next number after 5 should be 4 (odd column; 3 + 1 = 4).

7. **B**. The pattern is 3, 3, 2, 2, 1, 1. The pattern is that two columns have the same number of beads, then the number decreases by 1. There already have been 2 columns of 1 bead, so the next number after 1 should be 0 (1 – 1 = 0).

8. **A**. The pattern is 1, 3, 2, 4, 3, 5. There are two patterns here. The odd columns (1, 2, 3) increase by 1. The even columns (3, 4, 5) increase by 1, so the next number after 5 should be 4 (odd column; 3 + 1 = 4).

9. **A**. The pattern is 8, 4, 2, 1, 2, 4. At first, the number halves. After getting to 1, the number doubles, so the next number after 4 should be 8.

10. **C**. The pattern is 2, 2, 3, 3, 3, 4. The pattern is that there are the same number of columns as the number of beads, which is increasing by 1. Since there have not yet been 4 columns, the next number should be 4.

11. **C**. The pattern is 6, 4, 7, 6, 4, 7. The numbers 6, 4, and 7 repeat in that order, so the next number after 7 should be 6.

12. **B**. The pattern is 2, 4, 3, 4, 4, 4. There are two patterns here. The odd columns (2, 3, 4) increase by 1. The even columns (4, 4, 4) are all 4, so the next number after 4 should be 5 (4 + 1 = 5).

13. **B**. The pattern is 1, 1, 2, 1, 1, 1. 2 columns of 1 bead is followed by a column with 2 beads, so 3 columns of 1 bead should be followed by a column with 3 beads.

14. **A**. The pattern is 3, 5, 4, 4, 5, 3. There are two patterns here. The odd columns (3, 4, 5) increase by 1. The even columns (5, 4, 3) decrease by 1, so the next number after 3 should be 6 (odd column; 5 + 1 = 6).

15. **C**. The pattern is 6, 1, 4, 2, 2, 3. There are two patterns here. The odd columns (6, 4, 2) decrease by 2. The even columns (1, 2, 3) increase by 1, so the next number after 3 should be 0 (odd column; 2 – 2 = 0).

16. **D**. The pattern is 0, 6, 2, 3, 4, 0. There are two patterns here. The odd columns (0, 2, 4) increase by 2. The even columns (6, 3, 0) decrease by 3, so the next number after 0 should be 6 (odd column; 4 + 2 = 6).

17. **C**. The pattern is 1, 1, 2, 3, 3, 5. There are two patterns here. The odd columns (1, 2, 3) increase by 1. The even columns (1, 3, 5) increase by 2, so the next number after 3 should be 4 (odd column; 3 + 1 = 4).

18. **C**. The pattern is 8, 7, 1, 6, 5, 1. There are two patterns here. Every third column (1, 1) has 1 bead. The other columns (8, 7, 6, 5) decrease by 1. Since the next column is not a third column, it follows the pattern of the other columns, and the next number after 5 should be 4 (5 – 1 = 4).

NONVERBAL BATTERY
Explanations

Figure Matrices

1. **A**. The second figure is a larger version of the first figure. Choice A is a larger version of the triangle in the third figure.

2. **D**. The second figure is a vertically flipped version of the first figure. Choice D is a vertically flipped version of the third figure.

3. **C**. The second figure is the first figure rotated 90° clockwise. Choice C is the third figure rotated 90° clockwise.

4. **D**. The second figure is a smaller version of the first figure. Choice D is a smaller version of the pentagon in the third figure.

5. **A**. The second figure contains 2 of the first figure, joined at the edges. Choice A contains 2 of the third figure, joined at the edges.

6. **C**. The second figure is the first figure rotated 90° counterclockwise. Choice C is the third figure rotated 90° counterclockwise.

7. **D**. The second figure is the first figure stretched wider. Choice D is the third figure stretched wider.

8. **B**. The second figure is half of the first figure. Choice B is half of the third figure.

9. **B**. The second figure is a curved arrow pointing in the opposite direction (left) as the first figure is (right). Choice B is a curved arrow pointing in the opposite direction (down) as the third figure is (up).

10. **D**. The second figure is a horizontally flipped version of the first figure. Choice D is a horizontally flipped version of the third figure.

11. **D**. The second figure is the first figure with inverted shading. Choice D is the third figure with inverted shading.

12. **D**. The second figure shows the shape on the left side of the 3-D first figure. Choice D shows a circle, which is the shape on the left side of the 3-D third figure, which is a cylinder.

13. **B**. The second figure is the first figure with one triangular corner piece taken out. Choice B is the third figure with one triangular corner piece taken out.

14. **C**. The second figure shows the top shape in the first figure (plus sign) to the bottom left of the bottom figure (hexagon). Choice C shows the top shape in the third figure (pentagon) to the bottom left of the bottom figure (L shape).

15. **A**. The sequence of shapes in the first figure (circle, triangle, square) is reversed in the second figure (square, triangle, circle). The sequence of shapes in the third figure (diamond, square with cut corners, parallelogram) is reversed in choice A (parallelogram, diamond, square with cut corners).

16. **D**. The second figure shows the textures in each circle of the first figure moved to the adjacent counterclockwise circle. Choice D shows the textures in the squares of the third figure moved to the adjacent counterclockwise square.

17. **A**. The second figure shows the first figure with a hole shaped like a smaller version of the same figure rotated 180°. Choice A shows the third figure with a hole shaped like a smaller version of the same figure rotated 180°. C and D are incorrect because the interior shapes are not 180° rotations of the outer shapes.

18. **B**. The first figure shows, from outside to inside, an unshaded circle and a shaded diamond. The second figure shows the same figure but with an additional circle and inverted and alternating shading—gray, white, and gray. Furthermore, notice that each shape is touching the next larger figure at one or more points. The third figure shows an unshaded triangle and a shaded triangle inscribed inside it. Choice B is correct because it follows the pattern. C is incorrect, even though it follows the correct shading pattern because the shapes are not inscribed. D is incorrect because it doesn't follow the shading inversion and alternation.

Paper Folding

1. **A**. The paper is folded once, so there will be a total of 2 holes, as shown:

2. **B**. The paper is folded once, so there will be a total of 4 holes, as shown:

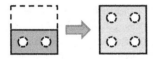

3. **A**. The paper is folded once, so there will be a total of 4 holes, as shown:

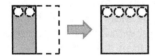

4. **B**. The paper is folded once, so there will be a total of 4 holes.

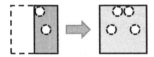

5. **D**. The paper is folded twice, so there will be a total of 4 holes, as shown:

6. **A**. The paper is folded twice, so there will be a total of 8 holes, as shown:

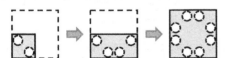

7. **C**. The paper is folded twice, so there will be a total of 8 holes, as shown:

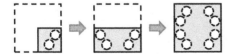

8. **D**. The paper is folded twice, so there will be a total of 12 holes, as shown:

9. **D**. The paper is folded once, so there will be a total of 4 holes, as shown:

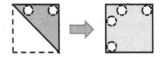

10. **A**. The paper is folded once, so there will be a total of 6 holes, as shown:

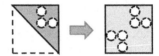

11. **C**. The paper is folded twice, so there will be a total of 4 holes, as shown:

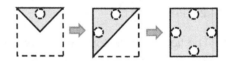

12. **B**. The paper is folded twice, so there will be a total of 8 holes, as shown:

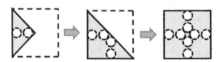

13. **D**. The paper is folded three times, so there will be a total of 8 holes, as shown:

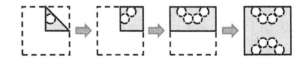

14. **D**. The paper is folded three times, so there will be a total of 8 holes, as shown:

Figure Classification

1. **D**. The figures in the top row are all circular with a sharp corner. Choice D is circular with a sharp corner.

2. **B**. The figures in the top row are all half shaded. Choice B is half shaded.

3. **D**. The figures in the top row all have parallel stripes. Choice D has parallel stripes.

4. **B**. The figures in the top row are all shapes with 2 lines of symmetry. Choice B is a shape with 2 lines of symmetry.

5. **B**. The figures in the top row all have 2 triangles and 1 square. Choice B has 2 triangles and 1 square.

6. **A**. The figures in the top row all have 2 lines that are parallel. Choice A has 2 lines that are parallel.

7. **C**. The figures in the top row are all shapes with 2 lines inside them. Choice C is a shape with 2 lines inside it.

8. **D**. The figures in the top row all have 2 shapes of the same color and a line separating them. Furthermore, none of the shapes in the top row have any curves or arcs; they are all composed of edges and line segments. Only choice D fits these criteria.

9. **B**. The figures in the top row are all circles with a line touching the outside of the circle at 2 points. Choice B is a circle with a line touching the outside of the circle at 2 points. Choice C doesn't work because it is not a circle.

10. **C**. The figures in the top row are all shapes with a hole of the same shape but smaller and flipped vertically. Choice C shows a trapezoid with a hole in the shape of the same trapezoid smaller and flipped vertically.

11. **B**. The figures in the top row are all hexagons with half of the hexagon being a shaded triangle, a white triangle, and a shaded triangle, with the white triangle in between the shaded triangles. Choice B is a hexagon with half being a shaded triangle, and white triangle, and a shaded triangle, with the white triangle in between the others.

12. **A**. The figures in the top row have 3 circles, each touching another circle at 1 point, with the smallest circle being the same shade as the largest circle. Choice A shows 3 circles, each touching another at 1 point, with the smallest circle being the same shade as the largest.

13. **A**. The figures in the top row show 3 of the same shape, but 2 are inside a box and are a different shade than the other shape. Choice A shows 3 stars, with 2 inside a box and of a lighter shade than the third star.

14. **D**. The figures in the top row all have a green arrow pointing to the square and a red arrow pointing away from it. Choice D shows a green arrow pointing to the square and a red arrow pointing away from it.

15. **D**. The figures in the top row are lines that intersect themselves once. Choice D shows a line that intersects itself once.

16. **A**. The figures in the top row are all fully shaded 3-D objects with at least 1 flat surface. Choice A shows a fully shaded rectangular prism, which has multiple flat surfaces.

17. **D**. The figures in the top row all have a large, striped plus sign and a small black shape. Choice D has a large, striped plus sign and a small black pentagon.

18. **A**. The colors of the squares in each figure of the top row are in the same clockwise sequence: starting at red, red – orange – yellow – green. Choice A has the same clockwise sequence.

Made in the USA
Las Vegas, NV
30 January 2025

17249390R00098